本教材为重庆财经学院（原重庆工商大学融智学院）2018年校级规划教

U1060296

财务会计与报告

Financial Accounting and Reporting

包燕萍 刘贤洲 程石 主编

西南财经大学出版社
中国·成都

图书在版编目(CIP)数据

财务会计与报告/包燕萍,刘贤洲,程石主编.—成都:西南财经大学出版社,2021.1(2023.8 重印)
ISBN 978-7-5504-4752-3

Ⅰ.①财… Ⅱ.①包…②刘…③程… Ⅲ.①财务会计—会计报告
Ⅳ.①F234.4

中国版本图书馆 CIP 数据核字(2021)第 000281 号

财务会计与报告

CAIWU KUAIJI YU BAOGAO

包燕萍　刘贤洲　程石　主编

策划编辑:张明星
责任编辑:李　才
责任校对:乔　雷
封面设计:张姗姗
责任印制:朱曼丽

出版发行	西南财经大学出版社(四川省成都市光华村街 55 号)
网　　址	http://cbs.swufe.edu.cn
电子邮件	bookcj@swufe.edu.cn
邮政编码	610074
电　　话	028-87353785
照　　排	四川胜翔数码印务设计有限公司
印　　刷	郫县犀浦印刷厂
成品尺寸	185mm×260mm
印　　张	11
字　　数	324 千字
版　　次	2021 年 1 月第 1 版
印　　次	2023 年 8 月第 2 次印刷
印　　数	2001— 3000 册
书　　号	ISBN 978-7-5504-4752-3
定　　价	35.00 元

1. 版权所有,翻印必究。
2. 如有印刷、装订等差错,可向本社营销部调换。
3. 本书封底无本社数码防伪标识,不得销售。

Contents

Chapter 1 Different Types of Business Organization

1.1 The Business World

Welcome to the business world. In this section, we are going to talk about what the business world looks like, to figure out what a business entity is, and what the different types of organizations are.

Everyone is overwhelmed in the business world, whether he/she recognizes it. What does the business world look like? Just imagine for one second. Can you live on the earth without any business? Probably not. You have to buy foods for everyday life and deal with the prices of different kinds of foods; you have to travel to work place, school, or a trip for holidays, and you have to consider the fares for the journey; you have to live in a place, and think about the housing prices. Just a few examples in our daily life indicate that, business exists among us all.

It is difficult to draw a picture of business world in the way as we do to have a map to understand the earth in a clear way. In this complicated business network, you may be a consumer, or a producer in the business cycle. To put it in a simple way, the business is dealing with "product" or "service". However, in this book, we are not

firm 公司
enterprise 企业
company 公司
corporation 法人(团体);公司

trying to describe much about how the business works, instead we are going to study how this "product" or "service" is described in the organization from the perspective of accounting, which can be considered as a business language for communicating information of that particular organization.

Sometimes we come across the term "firm", "enterprise", "company", and "corporation", and many of us may probably be crazy in identifying the meaning of each term and the differences between them, as they have similar translation in Chinese words "*Gongsi*". Yes, it is the particular organization dealing with different types of product or service in the business world. Let us first have a clear mind of those terms.

Academically, the terms "firm" and "enterprise" refer first and foremost to something that is physically, like production facilities, operations, and actions etc.

While the term "company" and "corporation", instead, refer to a legal phenomenon, to something that is created by the law.

A company or corporation does not exist naturally; they are created. Like a human being in the natural world he or she has a citizen identification in a country, an organization should have its legal rights and obligation in the society. In other words, any business organization must get its legal permission form the government where it locates before it starts its business activities.

But why does a company need to be created according to the laws in different countries? It is the main reasons for them to be protected and to protect consumers. Being protected, means that the certified company can get support and benefits from the government as long as it operates in accordance with the laws. From the point view of protecting, a certified company protects customers and suppliers by showing its trust and credits, which are important in the business process. No one would like to trade or have any contract with an organization without legal permission from government.

After an organization is created, it has its main objectives,

legal right 法定权利
obligation 义务
customers 顾客
suppliers 供应商
profit-oriented 以盈利为导向

non-governmental organization (NGOs) 非政府组织

which may be profit-oriented, or not-for-profit, to fulfill.

From the figure above, we can see the organizations are divided into two groups: one is called the profit-making sector (with its main purpose to seek profit from business activities), and the other is called the not-for-profit sector. This book will focus on the accounting process for the profit-making sector. In next section, more details about the three different business organizations will be discussed.

1.2 Different Types of Business Organization

In this section, some details of the different types of business organization are introduced by the basic distinction between their ownership, how they are financed and what the law requires of them.

1.2.1 Sole Traders

The term "sole trader", is a type of enterprise that is owned and run by one natural person and in which there is no legal distinction between the owner and the business entity.

There is no distinction between the person who is the sole trader and the business itself in the eye of the law. It means that, if the business is sued or owes money to creditors, it is the sole trader himself or herself who is legally responsible to settle these obligations.

Several characteristics of sole traders:

finance 金融；融资
accountable for 对……负责
unlimited responsibility 无限责任
discharge 履行（职责）
outstanding liabilities 未偿付的负债
duplicated 复制；复印
registration 登记

▶ The owner would normally be the main source of finance.

▶ The owner is in direct control of all elements.

▶ The owner is legally accountable for the finances of such as debts, loans, loss, etc. and has unlimited responsibility for all losses and debts. The owner carries the financial responsibility for all debts and/or losses suffered by the business, to the extent of using personal or other assets, to discharge any outstanding liabilities.

A sole trader may use a trade name or business name other than his, her, or its legal name. The business owner is required to register with the appropriate local authorities, who will determine that the name submitted is not duplicated by another business entity.

Furthermore, the business owner must complete a form submitted to the governing authority to acquire title as a "DBA" or "doing business as".

1.2.2 Partnership

A partnership entity is very much like a sole trader entity except that there must be at least two owners of the business. Partnerships often grow out of a sole trader entity, perhaps because more money needs to be put into the business or because the sole trader needs more help. For example, it is easier for several friends to start a new business together than one alone.

The partners should agree among themselves how much money or knowledge they will each bring to the business, what jobs they will do, how many hours they will work, and how the profits and losses will be shared (which may be different to the proportion of money they originally put into the business).

Normally, a partnership requires a written agreement between the partners. This written agreement must be submitted to the business registration government body along with the identity of the partners.

A partnership must abide by the following requirements:

√ Have 2 or more partners

√ Have a written partnership agreement

√ Have capital contributions subscribed to or actually paid by the partners

√ Have a name and a place of business for the partnership enterprise; and

√ Abide by any other conditions as provided for the law liabilities:

A partnership must pay all its debts with property contributed to the partnership by the partners.

If the partnership is a general one then the partners bear joint and several liabilities. A general partnership may be formed by general partners who bear unlimited joint and several liabilities for the debts of the partnership. The general partners share unlimited liabilities for the debt of the partnership.

abide 遵守
capital contributions 资本投入
subscribe 认购，签署
general partnership 普通合伙
joint and several liabilities 联合（连带）债务
incorporated 合并的；组成法人组织的
limited liability 有限责任
limited liability companies 有限责任公司
financial difficulties 财务困境

1.2.3 Company

When most people think of a company, they think of a vast public company, with hundreds or thousands of employees. However, many companies are very small, sometimes owned and run by just one person. So, what is the difference between a company and a sole trader, or a partnership?

The main characteristics of a company:

√ The company is a separate legal entity

√ Limited liability

From the perspective of law, a company is an entity that has separate existence from that of its owners. It is a separate legal "person". It follows that if a wrong is done to a company, it is the company, and not those who own the company's shares, that has the right to sue.

We are going to be primarily concerned with *limited liability companies*. The term "limited liability" means that the owners of such companies are required to finance the business only up to an agreed amount. Once they have contributed the agreed amount, they

public companies 上市公司
private companies 私营公司，非上市公司
dispersed 散布的，传播的
stock exchange 证券交易所

cannot be called on to contribute any more, even if the company gets into financial difficulties.

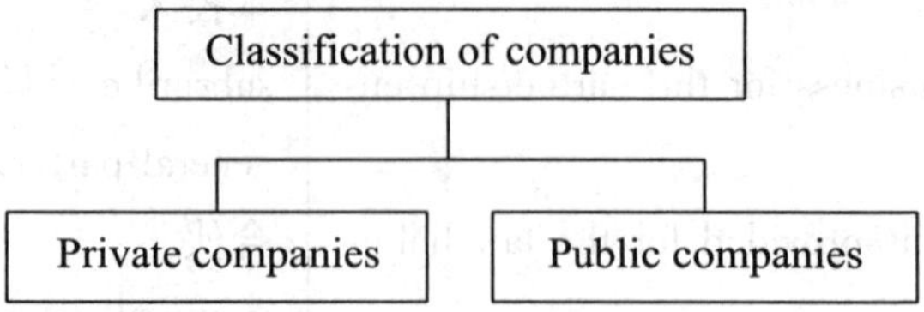

A privately held company (also named a private company) is a business company owned either by non-governmental organizations or by a relatively small number of shareholders or company members which does not offer or trade its company stock (shares) to the general public on the stock market exchanges.

A public company (also named as publicly traded company, publicly held company, publicly listed company) is a corporation whose ownership is dispersed among the general public in many shares of stock which are freely traded on a stock exchange.

Exercise 1

1. Single choice.

(1) Which of the following is not a characteristic of A Sole Trader?

A. The owner would normally be the main source of finance.

B. The owner has limited liability.

C. The owner is in direct control of all elements.

D. The owner carries the financial responsibility for all debts and/or losses suffered by the business

(2) Which of the following statement is incorrect?

A. A partnership entity is very similar to a sole trader entity except that there must be at least two owners of the business.

B. A partnership must pay all its debts with property contributed to the partnership by the partners.

C. The term "limited liability" means that the owners of such companies do not have liability to certain business activities.

D. A company is an entity that has separate existence from that of its owners.

2. Questions helpful to get a better understanding of this chapter.

(1) What is the meaning of profit-oriented?

(2) Can you name some of the NGOs in your country?

(3) What is meant by "limited liability"?

(4) What are the main differences between "sole trader" and "partnership"?

(5) What are the main characteristics of a company?

Broaden your perspective.

Warren Buffett

Who hasn't heard of Warren Buffett-one of the world's richest people, consistently ranking high on Forbes' list of billionaires?

Buffett is known as a businessman and philanthropist. But he's probably best known for being one of the world's most successful investors.

Warren Buffett was born in Omaha in 1930. He developed an interest in the business world and invested at an early age including in the stock market.

Buffett began his career as an investment salesperson in the early 1950s but formed the Buffett Partnership in 1956. Less than 10 years later, in 1965, he was in control of Berkshire Hathaway. In June 2006, Buffett announced his plans to donate his entire fortune to charity. Then, in 2010, Buffett and Bill Gates announced that they formed The Giving Pledge campaign to encourage other wealthy individuals to pursue philanthropy.

Buffett follows the Benjamin Graham school of value investing. Value investors look for securities with prices that are unjustifiably low based on their intrinsic worth.

Warren Buffett finds low-priced value by asking himself some questions when he evaluates the relationship between a stock's level of excellence and its price, such as:

√ Does the company perform well?

√ Does the company borrow money from creditors?

√ Is the management efficient and successful at controlling expenses to increase profit margins?

√ Is the company a public listed one, or a private one?

√ Does the company have competitive advantage?

Chapter 2 Financial Accounting Framework

Case Study

Before you get to learn the complicated accounting framework, it is better for you to have some ideas of how exactly a corporation works in the real setting. Here is a story related to accounting basics for you to read.

A person called Joe Peter would like to start a new business, because he sees the needs for a parcel delivery service in his community. Joe has researched his idea and has prepared a business plan that documents the potential success of his new business.

Joe has also met with an attorney to discuss the form of business he should use. Given his specific situation, they conclude that a corporation will be best. Joe decides that the name for his corporation will be Direct Delivery, Inc. The attorney also advises Joe on the various permits and government identification numbers that will be needed for the new corporation.

Joe is a hard worker and a smart man, but admits he is not comfortable with matters of accounting. He assumes he will use some accounting software, but wants to meet with a professional accountant before making his selection. He asks his banker to recommend a professional accountant who is also skilled in explaining accounting to someone without an accounting background. Joe wants to understand

accounting framework 会计框架

attorney 律师，代言人

professional accountant 职业会计师

the financial statements and wants to keep on top of his new business. His banker recommends Marilyn, an accountant who has helped many of the bank's small business customers.

At his first meeting with Marilyn, Joe asks her for an overview of accounting, financial statements, and the need for accounting software. Based on Joe's business plan, Marilyn sees that there will likely be thousands of transactions each year. She states that accounting software will allow for the electronic recording, storing, and retrieval of those many transactions. Accounting software will permit Joe to generate the financial statements and other reports that he will need for running his business.

Joe seems puzzled by the term transaction, so Marilyn gives him five examples of transactions that Direct Delivery, Inc. will need to record the following transactions:

1. Joe will no doubt start his business by putting some of his own personal money into it. In effect, *he is buying shares of Direct Delivery's common stock.*

2. Direct Delivery will need to buy a sturdy, dependable delivery vehicle.

3. The business will begin earning fees and billing clients for delivering their parcels.

4. The business will be collecting the fees that were earned.

5. The business will incur expenses in operating the business, such as a salary for Joe, expenses associated with the delivery vehicle, advertising, etc.

With thousands of such transactions in a given year, Joe is smart to start using accounting software right from the beginning. Accounting software will generate sales invoices and accounting entries simultaneously, prepare statements for customers with no additional work, write checks, automatically update accounting records, etc.

By getting into the habit of entering all the daily business transactions into his computer, Joe will be rewarded with fast and easy access to the specific information he will need to make sound business decisions.

earn 赚钱
bill 账单；收取账单费用
incur expense 产生费用
salary 工资
accounting software 会计软件
in a given year 在某个（给定的）年度
automatically 自动的

Marilyn tells Joe that accounting's "transaction approach" is useful, reliable, and informative. She has worked with other small business owners who think it is enough to simply "know" their company made $30,000 during the year (based only on the fact that it owns $30,000 more than it did on January 1). Those are the people who start off on the wrong foot and end up in Marilyn's office looking for financial advice.

income statement 利润表
balance sheet 资产负债表
statement of cash flows 现金流量表

If Joe enters all Direct Delivery's transactions into his computer, good accounting software will allow Joe to print out his financial statements with a click of a button. The three main financial statements are income statements, balance sheets, and statements of cash flows.

Learning Objectives

√ Understand the definition of accounting in the business.

√ Describe the roles of financial accounting.

√ Understand the major users of accounting information.

√ Explain the main elements of accounting.

√ Understand the meanings and the theory of accounting assumptions.

√ Describe the accounting principles.

2.1 What Is Accounting?

As a beginner of accounting, you may be very curious about what the word "accounting" means to you.

We begin with the word "count" first, which is used often in everyday language. We count something if we would like to know the exact number, and we count something if it means a lot to us.

count 计算
account 账号，账户
accountant 会计（人员）
accounting 会计（处理流程）

The word "account" refers to a record or narrative description of past events, while "accountant" is usually referred to someone who maintains and audits business account.

For business, accounting plays an essential role. It is said that, a strong company can attribute some of its success to its accounting. Without accounting, it would be hard to keep track of the business's finances and profitability, and its managers might not know exactly how much money is coming in or going out of the business.

A manager in a company wants to know about the financial situations in his company, and he asks the accountants to provide the information. That is one of the most important roles accounting plays in the business–to provide useful information.

It has been pointed out by large number of people that, accounting should be considered as a kind of business language, which can be communicated with different parties with their specific purposes. Accounting uses its own special terms and symbols to communicate financial information, and anyone who can interpret the specific information should learn the basic meaning of those terms and symbols.

It is also suggested that, accounting is a system used by businesses to track financial information, which may be helpful in making business decisions.

From an accountant's view, the process of accounting consists of recording all transactions that occur within a business and summarizing the information.

By a professional definition of accounting, experts hold that, accounting is an information system designed to record, classify and summarize systematically significant financial and other economic information about business firms, and analyses and interprets its results, with monetary unit as its main criterion.

2.2 What Role Does Accounting Play in a Company and How?

2.2.1 Providing a Service

One way of viewing accounting is as a form of service, which is provided by accountants to their "clients". These "clients" may be owners of the business, creditors, managers, suppliers, employees,

decision making 决策

accounting technique 会计技术

government agencies, general public, etc.

To meet those various information users' needs, accountants should provide a service with good quality in order to help these clients in decision making.

Generally speaking, this service relates to the process of providing information by using accounting techniques. Referring to the good quality of the service, many characteristics are considered. It is argued that accounting information should possess certain key qualities: relevance, reliability, comparability and understandability.

Relevance

Relevance is one of the most important features of good quality of the service provided by accountants.

Relevance means that the information may be relevant to the prediction of future events, which may have impact on the decision-making process. For example, in predicting how much profit is likely to be earned next year may be a key factor for those potential investors.

Relevance also means that the information is relevant in helping to confirm past events, for instance, in establishing how much profit was earned last year. The role of accounting in confirming past events is important because users often wish to check the accuracy of earlier predictions that they have made. The accuracy of earlier predictions may help users to judge the accuracy of current predictions. In other words, when an investor predicted a net income based on financial statement of previous period, and the predicted net income is proved in the current statement, it is said that the information provided is confirmed as the expectation by the investor. It is important, because the investor would predict again based on the current statement, or revise his expectation for the future.

Reliability

Accounting should be free from significant error or bias, which means that accounting information should be reliable and helpful to the users. It should be capable of being relied upon by managers to represent what it is supposed to represent.

accounting information characteristic 会计信息特征
relevance 相关性
prediction 预测
accuracy 准确性
reliability 可靠性
error or bias 错误或偏差

Though both relevance and reliability are very important, the problem that we often face in accounting is that information that is highly relevant may not be very reliable. Similarly, that which is reliable may not be very relevant.

Reliability is the extent to which information is verifiable, faithful and neutral. For example, the historical cost of a set of equipment to be reported in the balance sheet of a company is usually highly verifiable. The cost can be traced to an exchange transaction, the purchase of the equipment.

Reliability also assumes the information being relied on is neutral, with respect to parties potentially affected.

Comparability

Comparability, as one of the characteristics of accounting information, will enable users to identify changes in the business over time (for example, the trend in sales revenue over the past five years). It will also help them to evaluate the performance of the business in relation to similar businesses, for instance, companies in the same industry.

Comparability is achieved by treating items that are basically the same in the same manner for accounting purposes.

Comparability may also be enhanced by making clear the policies adopted in measuring and presenting the information.

Understandability

Accounting reports should be expressed in a way as clearly as possible and should be understood by those at whom the information is aimed.

verifiable 可验证的，可核实的
faithful 真实的
neutral 中立的，无偏的
historical cost 历史成本
comparability 可比性
evaluate 估值，评估
understandability 可理解性

2.2.2 Accounting as an Information System

Accounting is considered as the process of providing a "service" to different "clients". We would like to point out that accounting is as a part of the business's total information system. The information system is helpful for those who are inside and outside the business in their decision making concerning the allocation of scarce economic resources. To ensure that these resources are efficiently allocated, information users need economic information on which to base decision.

information system 信息系统
scarce economic resources 稀缺的经济资源
valid 有效的
recording 记录
analyzing 分析
interpreting 解读
reporting 报告

It is the role of the accounting system to provide this information.

The accounting information system should have certain features that are common to all valid information systems within a business.

These features are as follows:

1. Identifying and capturing relevant financial information;
2. Recording, in a systematic way, the information collected;
3. Analyzing and interpreting the information collected;
4. Reporting the information in a manner that suits the needs of users.

It is better to have a clear view of the accounting information system in the following figure.

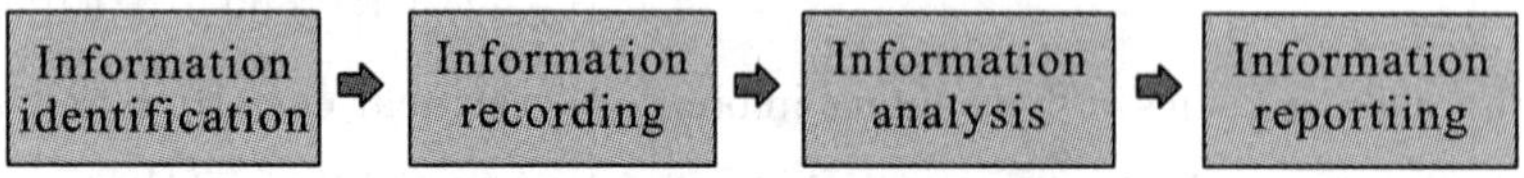

The accounting information system

The figure above shows that the accounting information system consists four parts of sequential stages. The first two stages are concerned with preparation, whereas the last two stages are concerned with using the information.

consist 包含
sequential 系列的

2.3 Objectives of Financial Reporting

For accounting information to be useful, the accountant must be clear FOR WHOM the information is being prepared, and FOR WHAT PURPOSE the information will be used. There are likely to be various groups of people (also known as information users) with an interest in a particular organization, in the sense of needing to make economic decision about it.

2.3.1 Who Are the Users of Accounting Information?

Almost anyone could be considered as a typical user of accounting information. In businesses, the finance department and executives are

typical 特别的，独特的
executive 执行人
owner 所有人
investor 投资人
creditor 债权人
supplier 供应商
employee 员工

primary information users, as it informs them how the business is performing financially and what the costs are in a company.

We can name a lot of different kinds of information users, such as managers, owners, investors, creditors, suppliers, employees, government agencies, community representatives, the general public, labor union, etc.

To make a clear picture of these various parties, the following figure may be helpful.

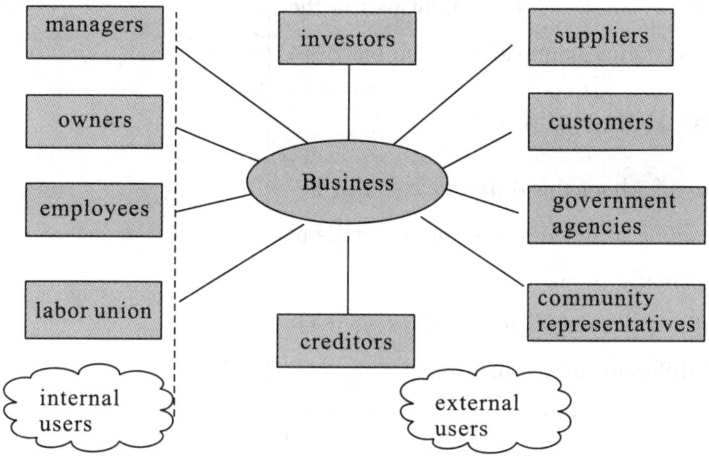

Main users of financial information relating to a business

As it is shown in the figure, we can simply divide the information users into two groups: those inside the company are considered as internal users, while those outside the company are referred to external users.

Internal users, such as owners, managers and other employees, are those who want to understand a company's performance. Managers make strategic and operational professional decisions all the time about how to make changes that can translate into success for the business. Personal decisions that benefit from accounting data include determining whether to look for a new job, deciding to take advantage of employee stock options or considering the likelihood of a year-end bonus.

In the above figure, the left part of the figure shows the internal users of accounting information in the business.

government agency 政府机构
community 社区
general public 社会公众
labor union 工会
financial interest 财务利益
day-to-day operation 日常经营活动
direct access 直接渠道

External users of accounting information are parties outside the operation of a business who use accounting and financial information in making important decisions. External users have a financial interest on the reporting company, but they are not involved in the day-to-day operations of the company. Examples include investors, creditors, regulatory authorities, suppliers, customers, and community representatives. Since these users do not have direct access to accounting information, they are given access to records by the business in the form of financial statements. In the above figure, we can see the right part of the figure shows the external users of accounting information in the business.

2.3.2 Decision Making for Different Users

Now that we have some ideas of whom the different users of accounting information are, we are going to discuss a bit more details of what kinds of information they are really interested in.

In order to make a clear outline, we would like to draw your attention to the decision making of different groups of users.

User group	Decisions or interested issues
Internal users	
managers	▶ Whether the performance of the business needs to be improved. ▶ Performance to date would be compared with earlier plans or some other "benchmark" to decide whether action needs to be taken. ▶ Whether there should be any change in the future plan. ▶ Will the firm be able to meet its debts as it matures? ▶ Is the amount owed by customers being collected rapidly? ▶ Are expenses too large in relation to sales revenues?
employees	▶ Whether to continue working for the company, and if so, whether to demand higher rewards for doing so. ▶ The future plans, profits and financial strength of the business are likely to be of particular interest when making their own decisions.
owners	▶ What are the risks and returns associated with the business? ▶ Owners may also be involved with decisions on rewarding senior managers.

(Continued)

User group	Decisions or interested issues
	External users
investors	▶ What are the company's cash flow prospects? ▶ Whether to invest more in the business or to sell all or part of the investment currently held.
creditors	▶ Whether to provide credit to the business. ▶ The assessment of the business's ability to pay for any debts.
suppliers	▶ The business's ability to pay for any goods or services provided. ▶ Whether to continue to supply the business, and if so, whether to supply on credit.
customers	▶ Whether to choose the goods or services of the business. ▶ The assessment of the quality of the products. ▶ The faithfulness of the enterprise in fulfilling warranty obligations.
government agencies	▶ Whether the business meets certain kinds of governmental regulations that apply. ▶ Whether the business should pay any taxes, and whether they are agreed with the financial reports.
community representatives	▶ Whether the business is socially responsible, for example does no harm to the environment. ▶ Whether to allow the business to expand its premises.

2.4 Elements of Financial Accounting

The whole point of accounting is to present a precise financial picture of your business operations. Generally speaking, the financial picture means the financial position of the business, as well as the operational results of the business. In order to make a clear picture of the business, accountants need to provide information accordingly by using different items related. In accounting, these items are classified, and they are "the building blocks with which financial statements are constructed". These elements are related to measuring performance and the financial position of the business.

Six elements of accounting are as follows:

- ◆ Asset
- ◆ Liability
- ◆ Owner's equity
- ◆ Revenue
- ◆ Expense
- ◆ Net income

accounting element 会计要素
assets 资产
liability 负债
owner's equity 所有者权益
revenue 收入
expense 费用
net income 利润

2.4.1 Asset

Assets refer to resources owned and controlled by the entity as a result of past transactions and events, from which future economic benefits are expected to flow to the entity.

A key characteristic of this definition is that an asset represents probable future economic benefits.

The meaning of "controlled" is also an important aspect of the definition of asset. Think about this – Are the employees of the business considered as the assets of a company? The employees certainly represent future economic benefits to the company, however, they are not owned or controlled by the company. Therefore, they are not qualified as assets.

In simple terms, assets are properties or rights owned by the business.

They may be classified as current or non-current.

Current assets are considered current if they are held for the purpose of being traded, expected to be realized or consumed within twelve months after the end of the period or its normal operating cycle (whichever is longer), or if it is cash.

Examples of current asset accounts are:

◆ Cash and cash equivalents–bills, coins, funds for current purposes, checks, cash in bank, etc.

◆ Receivables–accounts receivable (receivables from customers), notes receivable (receivables supported by promissory notes), interest receivable, due from employees (or advances to employees), and other claims

cash equivalent 现金等价物
receivables 应收（款）
inventories 存货
prepaid expense 预付款项（费用）
prepaid insurance 预付保险费
current asset 流动资产
non-current asset 非流动资产
current liability 流动负债

◆ Inventories-assets held for sale in the ordinary course of business

◆ Prepaid expenses-expenses paid in advance, such as prepaid rent, prepaid insurance, prepaid advertising, and office supplies

Non-current assets are assets that do not meet the criteria to be classified as current. Hence, they are long-term in nature-useful for a period longer that 12 months or the company's normal operating cycle.

Examples of non-current asset accounts include:

◆ Land-land area owned for business operations (not for sale)

◆ Building-such as office building, factory, warehouse, or store

◆ Equipment-machinery, furniture and fixtures (shelves, tables, chairs, etc.), office equipment, computer equipment, delivery equipment, and others

◆ Intangibles - long-term assets with no physical substance, such as goodwill, patent, copyright, trademark, etc.

2.4.2 Liability

Company assets come from two major sources - borrowings from lenders or creditors, and contributions by the owners. The first refers to liabilities; the second to capital.

Liabilities represent claims by other parties aside from the owners against the assets of a company.

Liabilities are probable future sacrifices of economic benefits arising from present obligations of particular entities to transfer assets or provide services to other entities in the future as a result of past transactions or events.

Just like assets, liabilities may be classified as either current or non-current.

Current liabilities are considered current if they are due within 12 months after the end of the balance sheet date. In other words, they are expected to be paid in the next year.

If the company's normal operating cycle is longer than 12 months, a liability is considered current if it is due within the operating cycle.

non-current liability 非流动负债

Current liabilities include:

√ Trade and other payables-such as accounts payable, notes payable, interest payable, rent payable, accrued expenses, etc.

√ Short-term borrowings-financing arrangements, credit arrangements or loans that are short-term in nature

√ Current tax liabilities - taxes for the period and are currently payable

Non-current liabilities are considered non-current if they are not currently payable, i. e. they are not due within the next 12 months after the end of the accounting period or the company's normal operating cycle, whichever is shorter.

In other words, non-current liabilities are those that do not meet the criteria to be considered current. Hah! Make sense? Non-current liabilities include:

√ Long-term notes, bonds;

√ Deferred tax liabilities; and

√ Other long-term obligations.

trade payables 应付账款

short-term borrowings 短期借款

long-term notes 长期应付票据

defferred tax 递延所得税

2.4.3 Owners' Equity

Owners' equity, also known as net assets or equity, refers to what is left to the owners after all liabilities are settled.

Simply stated, owners' equity is equal to total assets minus total liabilities, and is the residual interest in the assets of an entity.

Owners' equity can be increased by adding additional contributions to the business by owners or investors, or by realizing revenue from sales of goods and services. Likewise, owners' equity would be decreased by withdrawal made by owners, or distributing dividends for corporations.

The common items related to owners' equity are as follows:

√ Contributed capital-resulting from transfers of resource to a company by investors in exchange for ownership interest.

√ Retained earnings-retained earnings represent taxed profits that have not been distributed to shareholders.

Assets and liabilities are measured directly; equity is not. It is calculated by the accounting equation:

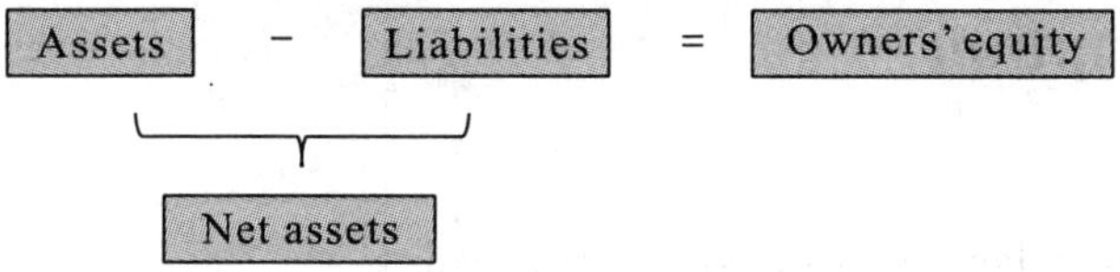

2.4.4 Revenue

Revenues are inflows or other enhancements of assets or settlements of liabilities from delivering or producing goods, rendering services, or other activities that constitute the entity's ongoing major, or central, operations.

A key characteristic is that revenues are inflows.

The business entity is acquiring something in exchange for providing goods and services to customers. Also, providing these goods and services represents a major operation of the business entity.

On the other hand, if selling one item is not part of the central operations of the business, but instead is only an incidental result of those operations, the inflow of assets would produce a gain rather than a revenue.

2.4.5 Expense

Expenses are outflows or other using up of assets or incurrences of liabilities during a period from delivering or producing goods, rendering services, or other activities that constitute the entity's ongoing major, or central, operations.

Expenses include ordinary expenses such as cost of sales, advertising expense, rent expense, salary expense, income tax, repair expense, etc.

2.4.6 Net Income (Net Loss)

The result of matching revenues with expenses refers to net income or profit. When revenues exceed expenses, net income

inflow（现金）流入
outflow（现金）流出
enhancement 增加，增强
render service 提供服务
constitute 构成，组成
ongoing major operation 主营业务
gain 利得
cost of sale 销售成本
advertising expense 广告费用
rent expense 租金费用
salary expense 工资费用
income tax 所得税
repair expense 维修费用

occurs; otherwise net loss occurs.

2.5 Accounting Assumption

Key accounting assumptions state how a business is organized and operates. They provide a structure to how business transactions are recorded.

Four accounting assumptions are:

Economic Entity Assumption

Going Concern Assumption

Accounting Period Assumption

Monetary Unit Measurement Assumption

2.5.1 Economic Entity Assumption

According to this assumption, the business is treated as a unit or entity apart from its owners, creditors, managers, and others.

In other words, the proprietor of an enterprise is always considered to be separate and distinct from the business which he controls. The assumption of the separate entity is applicable to all forms of business organizations.

All the transactions of the business are recorded in the books of the business from the point of view of the business.

For example, from a legal point of view, a body corporate is a separate entity and the sole trader and his business is regarded as one and the same thing.

But for accounting purposes, they are regarded as different entities. For recording the transactions, it is the business which is the entity and with which we are concerned.

The assumption of the business as a separate legal entity as distinct from its owners has been well accepted in relation to companies all over the world

In brief:

accounting assumption 会计假设

Economic Entity Assumption 会计主体假设

Going Concern Assumption 持续经营假设

Accounting Period Assumption 会计分期假设

Monetary Unit Measurement Assumption 货币计量假设

√ Only the business transactions and not the personal transactions of the proprietor are recorded and reported.

√ The personal assets of the owners or shareholders are not considered while recording and reporting the assets of the business entity.

√ Income is the property of the business assets distributed to owners.

property 资产
distribute 分配（给……）

2.5.2 Going Concern Assumption

It is also known as continuity assumption. According to this assumption, the enterprise is normally viewed as a going concern, i. e. continuing in operation for the foreseeable future.

It is assumed that the enterprise has neither the intention nor the necessity of liquidation or of curtailing materially the scale of its operations.

Please note that, it is because of the going concern assumption

√ that the assets are classified as current assets and non-current assets;

√ that the liabilities are classified as short-term liabilities and long-term liabilities.

√ that the unused resources are shown as unutilized costs (or unexpired costs), as against the break-up values, and as in the case of a liquidating enterprise. Accordingly, the earning power and not the break-up value evaluates the continuing enterprise.

According to accounting standards, if this concept is followed, this fact doesn't need to be disclosed in the financial statements since its acceptance and use are assumed.

In case this concept is not followed, the fact should be disclosed in the financial statements together with reasons.

A balance sheet is prepared under the assumption that the concern for which the statement is made will continue in operation.

If the going concern assumption is no longer valid for a company, then, the land held as an investment would be valued at its liquidation value; all prepaid assets would be completely written off

continuity 持续，连续性
the foreseeable future 可预测的未来
liquidation 破产，清算
curtailing 缩短，减少
written off 注销
the allowance for uncollectible accounts 计提的坏账准备

immediately; the allowance for uncollectible accounts would be eliminated.

2.5.3 Accounting Period Assumption

It is also known as periodicity assumption or time period assumption.

Life of a business often lasts many years and its activities go on without interruption over the years.

The most accurate way to measure the results of the enterprise activity would be the time of the enterprise's eventual liquidation. However, business, government, investors, creditors and so on cannot wait indefinitely so long for the information. They need information for their decision making.

According to this assumption, the economic life of an enterprise is artificially split into periodic intervals which are known as accounting periods, at the end of which an income statement and financial position statement are prepared to show the performance and financial position.

The use of this assumption further requires the allocation of expenses between capital and revenue.

That portion of capital expenditure which is consumed during the current period is charged as an expense to the income statement and the unconsumed portion is shown in the balance sheet as an asset for future consumption.

Truly speaking, measuring the income following the concept of the accounting period is more an estimate than factual since actual income can be determined only on the liquidation of the enterprise.

interruption 打断
indefinitely 无限期地
artificially 人为地
periodic intervals 周期性间隔
financial position 财务状况
capital expenditure 资本化支出

2.5.4 Monetary Unit Assumption

It is well accepted that, money is the common denominator. Money provides an appropriate basis for accounting measurement and analysis.

The money unit assumption underlines the fact that in accounting

common denominator 共同价值尺度
underline 强调
cash balance 现金账户余额

every worth-recording event, happening or transaction is recorded in terms of money.

In other words, a factor or an event which cannot be expressed in terms of money is not recorded in the account books. It should be disclosed in the notes if necessary.

This assumption increases the understanding of the state of affair of the business.

For example, if a business has a cash balance of \$7,000, a building containing 20 rooms, a piece of land of 2,000 square meters, 40 tables, 20 fans, 2 machines, one tone of raw material and so on...

Then in the absence of money measurement assumption the value of different types of assets cannot be measured by the simple method in addition.

But if they are expressed in monetary terms – \$7,000 cash, \$50,000 for building, \$200,000 for land, \$8,000 for tables, \$6,000 for fans, \$160,000 for machines, \$80,000 for raw material–It is possible to add them and use them for comparison or any other purpose.

2.6 Accounting Principles

Basic principles of accounting are essential and these are the general decision-making rules which govern the development of accounting techniques.

These principles guide how transactions should be recorded and reported.

On the basis of the four basic assumptions of accounting, the following basic principles of accounting have been developed:

Historical Cost Principle

Realization Principle

Matching Principle

Historical Cost Principle 历史成本原则
Realization Principle 实现原则
Matching Principle 配比原则
Full Disclosure Principle 全面披露原则
purchase 购买
acquire 采购，并购

The Full Disclosure Principle

2.6.1 Historical Cost Principle

According to this principle, an asset is ordinarily recorded in the accounting records at the price paid to acquire it at the time of its acquisition and the cost becomes the basis for the accounts during the period of acquisition and subsequent accounting periods.

Under this principle, all goods and services purchased by an enterprise are recorded at acquisition cost and appear on financial statement at cost, rather than the current market value.

The historical cost principle is used to reflect the amount of capital expended to acquire an asset, and is useful for matching against changes in profits or expenses relating to the asset purchased, as well as for determining past opportunity costs.

For example, ABC company purchased an equipment for the price of \$35,000 on January 1, 2019, thus the cost of the equipment should be \$35,000. Even though the market value of the equipment would be changed, the historical cost should be kept, until the operation intention of the company has changed.

Historical cost measurement provides relevant cash flow information and also is highly verifiable.

2.6.2 Realization Principle

accrual accounting model 权责发生制会计

recognize as a revenue 确认为收入

earnings process 实现收入的环节/流程

collectability 可收到

To begin with, we have to understand the accrual accounting model. Revenues are inflows of assets resulting from providing a product or service to a customer. At what point is this event recognized as a revenue and increase in assets? The realization principle requires that two criteria be satisfied before revenue can be recognized:

1) The earnings process is judged to be complete or virtually complete.

2) There is reasonable certainty as to the collectability of the asset to be received (usually cash).

The realization principle is the concept that revenue can only be recognized once the underlying goods or services associated with the revenue have been delivered or rendered, respectively.

The realization principle means that revenues are usually measured when they occurred and are earned, rather than in the period in which they are collected.

A crucial question for many companies is when to recognize revenue. Revenue recognition generally occurs when realized or realizable and when earned. This approach has often been referred to as the revenue recognition principle.

For example, Company A sells an equipment to Company B at the price of $20,000, and the equipment has been delivered according to the contract terms and conditions. Company A provides a trade credit for Company B that Company B could make the payment in 30 days. In this case, Company A's earning process is completed or virtually completed, but has not received the payment. According to the realization principle, the earnings process is judged to be complete, and there is reasonable certainty that Company B is going to make the payment, and Company A should recognize the revenue. In the accounting treatment for the activity, an asset of receivable is increased, and the revenue is also increased.

2.6.3 Matching Principle

When are expenses recognized? The matching principle states that expenses are recognized in the same period as the related revenues.

There is a cause-and-effect relationship between revenue and expense recognition in this definition.

In a given period, revenue is recognized according to the realization principle. And the matching principle then requires that all expenses incurred in generating that revenue also be recognized. Matching principle is usually used to measure expenses. It is required that all expenses measured should be matched to revenue.

In a business, expenses are necessary to earn revenue, or in other words, business incurs expenses in order to earn revenue.

cause-and-effect relationship 因果关系
straightforward 直接的
accounting period 会计期间
systematic 系统性的
rational allocation 合理分配
generate revenue 创造收益

Although the concept is straightforward, its implementation can be difficult. The difficulty arises in trying to identify cause-and-effect relationships. Many expenses are not incurred directly. Instead, the expenses are incurred to generate the revenue, but the association is indirect.

unfortunately 不幸地
salary 工资

According to this principle, the expenses incurred in an accounting period should be matched with the revenues recognized during that period.

An expense can be recognized

1) based on an exact cause-and-effect relationship between a revenue and expense event.

2) by associating an expense with the revenue recognized in a specific time period.

3) by a systematic and rational allocation to specific time period.

4) in the period incurred, without regard to related revenue.

For example, the cost of goods sold, or the cost of sale, is a direct cost incurred to generate the revenue from the sale.

Unfortunately, for most expenses there is no obvious cause-and-effect relationship between a revenue and expense event. In other words, the revenue event does not directly cause expenses to be incurred.

For instance, the monthly salary paid to an office worker is not directly related to any specific revenue event. In this setting, the employee provided services during the month. The asset (usually cash) used to pay the employee provides benefits to the company only for that one month and indirectly relates to the revenue recognized in that same period.

2.6.4 The Full Disclosure Principle

Do you still remember what the purpose of accounting is?

The purpose of accounting is to provide information that is useful to decision makers.

So, naturally, if there is accounting information not included in the primary financial statements that would benefit users, that infor-

decision maker 决策者
subjective 主观的
disclose 披露
information disclosure 信

mation should be provided too.

The full disclosure principle states that financial records should include all the information necessary for readers to understand those records. This is a largely subjective principle, but full disclosure doesn't mean that records should include irrelevant information.

The information disclosed according to this principle can appear in a variety of formats, including footnotes, appendices and schedules within financial statements.

This information can also be included outside of financial statements, such as in annual reports to government bodies, press releases, shareholder meetings and public interoffice communications. This means that, though the supplemental and explanatory information should be available, it doesn't have to be written alongside financial records.

Examples for full disclosure:

The notes to a company's financial statements will likely begin with a description of the company's significant accounting policies such as how and when revenues are recognized, how property is depreciated, how inventory and income taxes are accounted for, and more.

Other disclosures in the notes to the financial statements include the effects of new accounting pronouncements, details regarding earnings per share, receivables, advertising, leases, related-party transactions, income taxes, contingent liabilities, and much more.

息披露
a variety of 很多的
format 格式
footnote 脚注
appendices 附注
annual report 年报
press release 新闻发布
shareholder meeting 股东大会
supplemental 附加的
explanatory 可解释的
significant accounting policies 重要的会计政策
depreciated 折旧
earnings per share 每股收益
lease 租赁
related-party transaction 关联交易
contingent liabilities 或有负债

2.7 Cash Basis and Accrual Basis

Cash basis model and accrual basis model produce a periodic measure of performance that could be used by investors and creditors. The difference between cash and accrual accounting lies in the timing of when sales and purchases are recorded in your accounts. Cash accounting recognizes revenue and expenses only when money changes

cash basis 现金收付制
accrual Basis 权责发生制

hands, but accrual accounting recognizes revenue when it's earned, and expenses when they're billed (but not paid).

2.7.1 Cash Basis

The cash basis accounting produces a measure called net operating cash flow. This measure is the difference between cash receipts and cash disbursements during a reporting period from transactions related to providing goods and services to customers.

Net operating cash flow is very easy to understand and all information required to measure it is factual.

The cash basis of accounting recognizes revenues when cash is received, and expenses when they are paid. This method does not recognize accounts receivable or accounts payable.

The cash method is also beneficial in terms of tracking how much cash the business actually has at any given time. You can look at your bank balance and understand the exact resources at your disposal.

2.7.2 Accrual Basis

Under the accrual basis, revenues and expenses are recorded when they are earned, regardless of when the money is actually received or paid. This method is more commonly used than the cash method.

The upside is that the accrual basis gives a more realistic idea of income and expenses during a period of time, therefore providing a long-term picture of the business that cash accounting can't provide.

The downside is that accrual accounting doesn't provide any awareness of cash flow; a business can appear to be very profitable while in reality it has empty bank accounts. Accrual basis accounting without careful monitoring of cash flow can have potentially devastating consequences.

Example for cash basis model:

The following table illustrates the net operating cash flows for Company C during its first 3 years of operations. Sales on credit means that the company sold products to its customers, but the company has not yet received all payment. In this example, the company generated \$ 10, 000 sales every year, but the cash received is not equal to the sales. The company prepaid \$ 6, 000 for the next 3 years' rent. The company paid \$ 5, 000 every year for the employees. The company also incurred \$ 1, 000 other expenses every year, but it paid \$ 500 for the first year, \$ 1, 500 for the 2nd year, and \$ 1, 000 for the 3rd year. From the following table, we can see over the 3 years period, Company C generated a positive net operating cash flow of \$ 6, 000.

unit: \$

	Year 1	Year 2	Year 3	Total
Sales (on credit)	10, 000	10, 000	10, 000	30, 000
Net operating cash flows				
Cash receipts from customers	5, 000	12, 500	12, 500	30, 000
Cash disbursement:				
Prepayment of 3 years' rent	6, 000	0	0	6, 000
Salaries to employees	5, 000	5, 000	5, 000	15, 000
Other expenses	500	1, 500	1, 000	3, 000
Net operating cash flow	6, 500	6, 000	6, 500	19, 000

Let us see what happens if we use accrual accounting model for the same company.

The accrual accounting model measures the entity's accomplishments and resources used during the period, regardless of when the cash is received or paid. The revenue for each year is \$ 10, 000 though the company has not received the cash. The prepaid rent for 3 years, which was \$ 6, 000, should be recognized \$ 2, 000 in each year for the rent is beneficial for the 3 years' uses. The same theory can be applied to the other expenses.

Thus, the net income of \$ 2, 000 for Year 1 appears to be a reasonable predictor of the company's cash-generating ability.

Net cash flow for accrual basis model unit: $

	Year 1	Year 2	Year 3	Total
Revenue	10, 000	10, 000	10, 000	30, 000
Expenses				
Rent	2, 000	2, 000	2, 000	6, 000
Salary	5, 000	5, 000	5, 000	15, 000
Other expenses	1, 000	1, 000	1, 000	3, 000
Total expense	8, 000	8, 000	8, 000	24, 000
Net income	2, 000	2, 000	2, 000	6, 000

The following table shows us the advantages and disadvantages of the two methods above.

Advantages and disadvantages of both methods

	Advantages	Disadvantages
Cash basis	Its simplicity since it only accounts for cash paid or received. Tracking cash flow of a company is also easier with the cash method.	It might overstate the health of a company that is cash-rich but has large sums of accounts payables that far exceed the cash on the books and the company's current revenue stream. An investor might conclude the company is making a profit when in reality the company is losing money.
Accrual basis	It includes accounts receivables and payables and, as a result, is a more accurate picture of the profitability of a company, particularly in the long term. The accrual method records all revenues when they are earned and all expenses when they are incurred.	It doesn't track cash flow and, as a result, might not account for a company with a major cash shortage in the short term, despite looking profitable in the long term. It can be more complicated to implement since it's necessary to account for items like unearned revenue and prepaid expenses.

Exercise 2

1. **For each of the items below, identify the appropriate financial statement element or elements.**
   a) Obligation to transfer cash or other resources as a result of a past transaction.
   b) Inflow of an asset from providing goods or services.
   c) An item owned by the company representing probable future benefits.
   d) Outflow of an asset related to the production of revenue.
   e) The owner's residual interest in the assets of a company.
2. **The followings are the basic assumptions, and accounting principles. Please translate them into Chinese words.**
   a) Economic entity assumption
   b) Going concern assumption
   c) Periodicity assumption
   d) Monetary unit assumption
   e) Historical cost principle
   f) Realization principle
   g) Matching principle
   h) Full-disclosure principle
3. **Single choice exercises.**
   1) The primary objective of financial accounting is to (   ).
      A. provide information
      B. book keeping
      C. record expenses
      D. finance and invest
   2) The objective of the matching principle is to (   ).
      A. provide full disclosure
      B. recognize the expenses in the period that related revenue are recognized
      C. provide timely information to the decision maker
      D. promote comparability of the financial statements in different periods
   3) Which of the following item is not an asset? (   ).
      A. Receivables　　B. Cash
      C. Inventory　　D. Long-term note

4. Questions for review of key topics in this chapter.

1) What is the function and primary focus of financial accounting?

2) Who would be the internal users of accounting information?

3) Who would be the external users of accounting information?

4) List the key accounting assumptions and explain the meaning of each assumption.

5) Discuss the terms of "relevance" and "reliability", and use examples to illustrate its meanings in relation to financial accounting information.

6) What is the going concern assumption?

7) What are the major accounting principles that guide accounting practice?

8) Explain the difference between cash basis model and accrual basis model.

Broaden your perspective

Difference Between Book-Keeping and Accounting

Many people possess erroneous concepts regarding book-keeping and accounting.

Actually, they are neither synonymous nor two different subjects.

Book-keeping and accounting play separate roles only in ascertaining final results of financial transactions.

In fact, these may be termed as two steps or stages of the same subject.

Book-keeping is a primary or practical aspect and accounting is a final or theoretical aspect of accounting.

Accounting starts from where book-keeping ends.

In other words, it can be said that book-keeping is the basis of accounting and the accounting is the structure based on book-keeping.

Apparently, any basic difference between book-keeping and accounting is not marked. The difference which is marked by book-keeping and accounting is very narrow.

Even in practice, it is difficult to draw a clear demarcation between activities of book-keeping and accounting.

Book-Keeping	Accounting
The art of recording of all financial transactions supported by valid documents in a particular method is called book-keeping.	Accounting is the task of preparing financial statements with the help of ledger balances and analyzing and interpreting the financial statements and also communicating the information to the users.

(Continued)

Book-Keeping	Accounting
Book-keeping is the primary stage of the whole accounting process. In this stage, journalizing, recording and balancing are made.	Accounting is the second or final stage of the whole accounting process. In this stage financial statements are prepared with a view to finding out financial results and exhibiting financial position and communicating the information to the management and other interested parties after necessary analysis and interpretation.
A person (persons) concerned with book-keeping is (are) called a book-keeper (book-keepers).	A person (persons) concerned with the final stage of accounting is (are) called an accountant (accountants).
The task of book-keeping is to record the transactions. So, in this aspect theoretical knowledge is more important.	The task of an accountant is to prepare, present and communicate information. So, in this aspect knowledge of application is more important.
Employees who perform book-keeping tasks are considered as lower category employees in the organogram of the organization.	Accountants possess the status of high officials. That is why in some cases the accountants enjoy the status of financial advisers or directors.
All primary activities-identification, recording and posting of transactions are included in book-keeping.	Preparation of trial balance with the help of ledger account balances to prove the arithmetical accuracy of the ledger accounts and preparation of financial statements taking into consideration necessary adjustments and interpretation and analysis are the functions of accounting.
A book-keeper might not be highly qualified as he is not supposed to have knowledge of other relevant disciplines.	An accountant is to have professional discretionary power and the knowledge of various laws apart from the knowledge of accounting. It may be mentioned that the above-mentioned differences between book-keeping and accounting are theoretical. But in practice drawing demarcation between these two are not feasible because in most of the organizations the same persons perform both types of tasks.

Chapter 3 An Introduction to the Basic Financial Statement

Case Study

Do you remember the case of Joe Peter starting a new business in parcel delivery? His chief accountant Marilyn suggests him the accounting software to help record financial business information, generate sales invoices and accounting entries, and prepare financial statements simultaneously through electronic progress. It sounds truly simple and highly efficient. Even with the help of the software, we are not saying we should completely rely on it. We need to understand the fundamental principle and rules of accounting.

financing 筹资业务
purchasing 采购业务

When Joe's company provides service to their clients, they need to recognize the revenue and relating cost. We take such case for instance. The question is: how do we record such transaction? How do we journalize it and post it? How do we adjust them to form a formal financial statement? And what should the financial statements be like?

Learning Objectives

The financial information about the company is always given through financial statements, so that we need to learn to analyze those financial statements. Before that, it is necessary to understand how the financial statements are prepared, what rules we should comply with, and how the transactions and events are recorded along the time.

In this chapter, we will meet the following objectives:

√ To record financial information through debit and credit complying with double-entry rules.

√ To understand T-accounts.

√ To journalize, post and adjust financial information in working sheets.

√ To prepare basic financial statements.

3.1 What Are Financial Statements?

Throughout time, an entity will carry out a series of activities such as financing, purchasing, selling and expensing. It is impossible to impress information users with tons of words and sentences regarding those activities and how the business is working. Hence financial statements are prepared to convey those business activities and financial performance by a company. Basic financial statements include:

√ Balance sheet

√ Income statement

√ Cash flow statement

We will mainly introduce the former two statements in the coming parts.

T accounts and Debit & Credit

An account is a place or location within an accounting system in which the increases and decreases in a specific asset, liability, owner's equity, revenue or expenses are recorded and stored. All the financial transactions in a certain entity should be recorded, and these accounts are used to summarize the financial transactions, and then the balances of these accounts flow into financial statement-the balance sheet, the income statement, the statement of cash flow and the statement of owner's equity.

balance sheet 资产负债表

income statement 利润表

cash flow statement 现金流量表

T-accounts T 形账户

debit 借记

credit 贷记

double-entry book-keeping 复式记账

◎T 形账户左边为借方，右边为贷方。金额计入左边称之为"借记"，金额计入右边称之为"贷记"。[1]

① More Chinese explanations, marked with "◎" ahead, are offered for a better understanding. —The editor

Accounts are the fundamental records used to summarize changes, the increase and decrease, in assets, liabilities and owner's equity. They will finally be brought into and shown in different financial statement element correspondently.

A T-account is an informal term for a set of financial records that use double-entry book-keeping. The term T-account describes the appearance of the book-keeping entries. A simple form of the T-account contains three parts:

(1) an account title, which describes the name of the item recorded in the account;

(2) a space for recording increases in the amount of the item, in monetary terms;

(3) a space for recording decrease in the amount of the item, in terms of money as well. Transactions are entered in T accounts with following rules:

a. Increases in the amount of an item are recorded on one side of the space, while the decreases entered on the other side.

b. The account balance is determined by subtracting the total decreases from the total increases.

The left side of the account is called the debit side, and the right side of the account is called the credit side. Amounts entered on the left side are called "debits or charges to the account", and the account is said to be debited or charged. Amounts entered on the right side are called "credits to the account", and the account is said to be credited.

assets accounts 资产类账户

Following is the example of T-account:

liability accounts 负债类账户

Account title

Left side Debit Side	Right side Credit Side

owner's equity accounts 权益类账户

The accounts are grouped into 6 categories in order to show what type of account is affected and whether debits or credits should be recorded. The 6 categories of accounts are assets, liabilities, owner's equity, revenues, expenses, and owner's withdrawals. We will in-

capital accounts 资本账户

troduce all these six groups of accounts respectively.

Asset accounts

Asset accounts carry their balances forward from one period to the next. Examples of asset accounts include cash, receivables, prepaid expenses (rent, taxes, supplies), equipment, buildings, land, etc. The recording of asset account on the left side shows the increases, and that on the right side presents the decreases.

Asset accounts

Debit (Increases)	Credit (Decreases)

Liability accounts

Liability accounts as well carry the balances forward from one period to the next. Examples of liability accounts include payable, unearned revenues and other liabilities (unpaid wages, taxes and interests). The recording of liability account on the left side shows the decreases, and that on the right side shows the increases.

withdrawals accounts 支付账户

Liability accounts

Debit (Decreases)	Credit (Increases)

revenue and expense accounts 收入与支出账户

Owner's equity accounts

Owner's equity accounts carry the balances forward from one period to the next. The owner's equity accounts can be divided into four separate accounts - capital, withdrawals, revenues and expenses.

Capital accounts

Capital accounts record the original investment and any permanent additional increases or decreases in owner's capital. The increase of the account is shown on the right side and the decrease of the account is shown on the left side.

Capital accounts

Debit (Decreases)	Credit (Increases)

Withdrawal accounts

Withdrawal accounts reflect how the owners withdraw the earnings of the company's residuals. It is definitely not the regular expenses of the company, such as salary paid to the employees. The increase of the account is shown on the left side and the decrease of the account is shown on the right side.

Withdrawal accounts

Debit (Increases)	Credit (Decreases)

Revenue and expense accounts

A business generates revenue when it exchanges goods or services with its customers in return for money or other assets. A business incurs expenses by exchanging its assets for goods and services it needs to generate revenue. A business realizes net income or profit if its revenues exceed expenses. If its expenses exceed revenues, the business incurs a loss. The income statement accounts remain the balances only during an accounting period, and will not be carried forward to the next. By the end of the period, the net profit or loss will be transferred to the equity accounts.

How do the increases and decreases influence the account?

Let's think about it in this way. The increase in revenue will cause the increase in capital, and we already know that the increase in capital will be recorded on the right side, so that the increase in revenue will be recorded on the right side. Accordingly, the expense will result in the decrease in capital, and will as well be shown on the left side of the account.

Revenue accounts

Debit (Decreases)	Credit (Increases)

Expense accounts

Debit (Decreases)	Credit (Increases)

Examples of revenue accounts are revenue from sales, rent earned, interest earned, etc.

Examples of expense accounts include salary expense, rent expense, advertizing expense and insurance expense and so on.

3.2　Double Entry Rule

Double Entry Rule 复式记账制度。任何业务的发生都会影响至少两个账户，所以在引起 一个账户金额变化的同时会引起另一个账户金额的变化。

Double entry accounting is a system of accounting in which every transaction has a corresponding positive and negative entry (debits and credits).

The double entry system of book-keeping is based on the fact that every transaction has two parts and that this will therefore affect two ledger accounts.

Every transaction involves a debit entry in one account and a credit entry in another account. This means that every transaction must be recorded in two accounts: one account will be debited because it receives value and the other account will be credited because it has given value. The transactions are recorded in the accounts following a very important accounting equation:

Assets = Liabilities + Owner's equity

Combined with the contents of T accounts we've introduced above, the debit-credit rules can be depicted as follows:

Assets			Liabilities			Owner's equity	
Debit (increase)	Credit (decrease)	=	Debit (decrease)	Credit (increase)	+	Debit (decrease)	Credit (increase)

Whether hand written or computerized, the ledger contains accounts of each asset and liability of the business and of the capital (amount invested) of the owner, and a separate account is kept for every item involved in business dealings.

The double entry system requires two entries for each transaction: a debit and a credit. Any purchases, such as raw materials or assets, as well as any payments from customers, must all be recorded in two places in the ledger under this system.

For example:

①John's business purchases $1,500 of raw materials from a supplier, which he will use to develop products that he will then sell to his customers. When he records this under the double entry system, he would debit his inventory account as an asset, and credit his cash account.

Dr. Inventory	1,500
Cr. Cash	1,500

②John runs a carpentry business and invoices a customer a dining table for $800. This transaction would be recorded as: A debit of $800 in his accounts receivable, and a credit of $800 to his revenue account.

More detailed accounts would also include a double entry approach to manage inventory and cost of goods sold (COGS): $500 debit to the COGS account, and $500 credit to the inventory account. These entries would allow John to better track his total profit, as the following equation illustrates.

Dr. Receivables	800
Cr. Revenue	800
Dr. Cost	500
Cr. Inventory	500

Let's take some examples for practice so that we can have further understanding on this part. Try to finish the double entry for each of the following transactions:

(1) Millie Co. issued on Dec. 2, 2015 capital share with a total of par value $170,000

Dr. Cash	170,000
Cr. Capital Stock	170,000

(2) Purchased for cash a piece of land on Dec. 5, as long-term investment $50,000.

Dr. Land	50,000

◎比如，John花1 500美元购买原材料，该项业务会引起现金（一项资产）的减少以及原材料（另一项资产）的增加。两项都是资产类项目，一增一减，资产负债表仍然是平衡的。

raw materials 原材料
carpentry 木工

accounts receivable 应收账款
revenue 收入
inventory 存货
COGS 销售成本
par value 股票价格；票面价值

Cr. Cash 50, 000

(3) Purchased on Dec. 6 equipment for cash $ 20, 000.

Dr. Equipment 20, 000

Cr. Cash 20, 000

(4) Purchased on Dec. 7 manufacturing machines for cash $ 10, 000.

Dr. Machine 10, 000

Cr. Cash 10, 000

(5) Purchased inventory on Dec. 8 on account for $ 200, 000.

Dr. Purchase 200, 000

Cr. Accounts Payable 200, 000

(6) On Dec. 10 made sales of merchandise to customers on account for $ 180, 000.

prepaid rent 预付租金

Dr. Accounts Receivable 180, 000

notes receivable 应收票据

Cr. Sales 180, 000

(7) On Dec. 11, paid cash $ 5, 000 for 3 months rent expenses in advance.

Dr. Prepaid Rent 5, 000

Cr. Cash 5, 000

(8) Paid on Dec. 13 cash $ 60, 000 for inventory goods on account.

Dr. Accounts Payable 60, 000

Cr. Cash 60, 000

(9) On Dec. 19, collection from customers $ 150, 000, of which $ 100, 000 cash and $ 50, 000 note with one-month period and 10% interest rate.

posting and journalizing 记账与过账

Dr. Cash 100, 000

Notes Receivable 50, 000

Cr. Accounts Receivable 150, 000

(10) On Dec. 22, paid other expenses $ 8, 000 in cash.

Dr. Other expenses 8, 000

trial balance 试算平衡

Cr. Cash 8, 000

(11) Made sales on Dec. 24 for cash $ 100, 000.

the book of original entry

Dr. Cash 100, 000

Cr. Sales 100, 000

(12) Paid salaries $ 42, 000 to employees on Dec. 26.

Dr. Salary expenses 42, 000

Cr. Cash 42, 000

原始分录账

ledger accounts 分类账 账户

subsidiary ledger 明细分类账

general ledger 总分类账

3.3 Journalizing and Posting

In accounting and book-keeping, a journal is a record of financial transactions in order by date. In practice, according to the double-entry accounting, transactions are first recorded in a journal, and it is sometimes called the book of original entry.

After the transaction has been recorded in the journal, the changes of credit and debit in the individual accounts are entered in the corresponding ledger accounts, both in subsidiary and general ledger accounts.

Try to finish the January journal of Millie Co. based on the information above.

Millie Company Journal unit: $

Date	Account Title & Explanation	Ref.	Debit	Credit
12.02	Cash		170, 000	
	Capital Stock			170, 000
12.05	Land		50, 000	
	Cash			50, 000
12.06	Equipment		20, 000	
	Cash			20, 000
12.07	Machine		10, 000	
	Cash			10, 000
12.08	Purchases		200, 000	
	Accounts Payable			200, 000

(Continued)

Date	Account Title & Explanation	Ref.	Debit	Credit
12. 10	Accounts Receivable		180, 000	
	Sales			180, 000
12. 11	Prepaid Rent		5, 000	
	Cash			5, 000
12. 13	Accounts Payable		200, 000	
	Cash			200, 000
12. 19	Cash		100, 000	
	Notes Receivable		50, 000	
	Accounts Receivable			150, 000
12. 22	Other Expenses		8, 000	
	Cash			8, 000
12. 24	Cash		100, 000	
	Sales			100, 000
12. 26	Salary Expenses		42, 000	
	Cash			42, 000
	Total		619, 000	619, 000

trial balance 试算平衡。期末对试算平衡表进行必要的调整。

3. 4 Trial Balance

unadjusted trial balance 未调整的试算平衡

After the Journal has been finished, an unadjusted trial balance is prepared. The trail balance proves the equality of the debit and credit entries in the company's accounting system. It is a two-column schedule listing the names and balances of all the accounts in the order in which they appear in the ledger, and the debit balances are listed in the left-hand column and the credit balances in the right-hand column. The total of the two columns should agree.

the equality of the debit and credit entries 借方和贷方分录相等（平衡）

Continue with the Millie Co. example. We can prepare the trial balance based on the journal prepared above.

Millie Company Trial Balance　　unit：$

Account Title	Debit	Credit
Cash	175, 000	
Notes Receivable	50, 000	
Prepaid Rent	5, 000	
Accounts Receivable	30, 000	
Land	50, 000	
Equipment	30, 000	
Accounts Payable		
Capital Stock		170, 000
Sales		280, 000
Purchases Salary	60, 000	
Expenses Other	42, 000	
Expenses Total	8, 000	
Total	450, 000	450, 000

accrued revenues 应计收益。对于一些收入，虽然在当前会计期间尚未收到，但是按照权责发生制，应归属于当前会计期间的，应该计入当前会计期间。

end-of-period adjusting 期末账项调整

3.5 End-of-Period Adjusting

accrued expenses 应计费用。对于一些费用，虽然在当前会计期间尚未发生，但是按照权责发生制，应归属于当前会计期间的，应该计入当前会计期间。

According to the accrual-basis principal and matching principal, all revenues earned and all expenses incurred during the same period must be reported regardless whether cash relating to revenues or expenses is received or paid. Hence it is necessary to make the adjusting entries at the end of the period. Normally, we should consider the accrued revenues, accrued assets, accrued expenses, accrued liabilities, unearned revenues and prepaid expenses.

3.5.1 Accrued Revenues (or Accrued Assets)

Accrued revenues are revenues that have been earned but have not been recorded in the accounts, including the fees for services that an attorney has provided but has not billed to the client at the end of the period, unbilled commissions by a travel agent, accrued interest on notes receivable, and accrued rent on property rented to others and so on. In such cases, we need to increase revenues in credit and assets in debit.

(13) At the end of the year, Millie Co. had already realized interest income $ 150. The adjusting entry is:

Dr. Interest Receivable 150

Cr. Interest Income 150

3.5.2 Accrued Expenses

Accrued expenses are the expenses that have been incurred but have not been recorded in the accounts, including an accrued interest on notes payable at the end of a period, accrued utility expenses and taxes, amortization of depreciation expenses, etc. In this situation, we should make adjusting entries to increase expenses in debit and increase liabilities or accumulated depreciation in credit.

(14) For example, the employees' salaries in Millies Co. were paid up to Dec. 26, those from Dec. 27 to the end of period have accrued on Dec. 31 and should be adjusted as:

Dr. Salary Expenses 3,000

Cr. Salary Payable 3,000

3.5.3 Unearned Revenues

Unearned revenues are the revenues that are recorded before and have become realized as time passes. This part of revenues must be assigned to the current period, in the period in which it realized.

(15) Millie Co. received on Dec. 21 (unearned) rent income for two months $ 600, from Dec. 21, 2017 to Feb. 20, 2018. On Dec. 31, 2017, the rent income for 10 days $ 100 ($ 600/2/3 = $ 100), which should be realized in current period. The increase of revenue should be recorded in credit side.

Dr. Unearned Rent Income 100

Cr. Rent Income 100

3.5.4 Prepaid Expenses

Prepaid expenses are the expenses that are paid before and have

unearned revenues 未实现收入。对于以前会计期间收到的款项，若不满足收入确认条件，则不可确认收入，应计入未实现收入科目，当其在后期满足收入确认条件后，再转入收入科目。

prepaid expenses 待摊费用（预付）。对于支付的费用，按权责发生制不属于当期的，应计入待摊费用科目，于其真正归属期费用化。

current period 当前会计期间

rent income 租金收入

become actual expenses as time passes. Just like unearned revenue, this part of prepaid expenses must be included in the current period as it is realized. Examples are prepaid rent, office supplies and prepaid insurance.

(16) Millie paid rent \$1,600 for two months starting from Dec. 15, 2017, half month's rent expenses \$400 (\$1,600/2/2 = \$400) should be realized in current period.

Dr. Other expenses 400

Cr. Prepaid Rent 400

Work Sheet

unit: \$

Account Title	Trial Balance		Adj. Entries		Adj. Trial Balance	
	Credit	Debit	Credit	Debit	Credit	Debit
Cash	35,000				35,000	
Notes Receivable	50,000				50,000	
Prepaid Rent	5,000			400	4,600	
Accounts Receivable	30,000				30,000	
Land	50,000				50,000	
Equipment	30,000				30,000	
Accounts Payable						
Unearned Rent Income			100		100	
Capital Stock		170,000				170,000
Sales		280,000				280,000
Purchases	200,000				200,000	
Salary Expenses	42,000		3,000		45,000	
Other Expenses	8,000		400		8,400	
Total	450,000	450,000				
Interest Receivable			150		150	
Interest Income				150		150
Salary Payable				3,000		3,000
Rent Income				100		100
Total			3,650	3,650	453,250	453,250

closing entry 结账

3.6 Closing Entry

real or permanent accounts 永久性账户

nominal or temporary accounts 暂时性账户

income summary 收益汇总（类似于“利润分配”）

retained earnings 留存收益

The balance sheet accounts are called real or permanent accounts in the sense that they are not closed to a zero balance at the end of the accounting period. In contrast, the income statement accounts are called nominal or temporary accounts because they are closed out to a zero balance at the end of each accounting period. Closing entries are journal entries made at the end of an accounting period which transfer the balances of temporary accounts to permanent accounts. Closing entries are based on the account balances in an adjusted trial balance. Closing entries are as well better explained via an example.

(17) Closing the revenue accounts to the Income Summary accounts.

Dr. Sales	280,000
Interest Income	150
Rent Income	100
Cr. Income Summary	280,250

(18) Closing the expense accounts and the Cost of Goods Sold account.

Dr. Income Summary	253,400
Cr. Cost of Goods Sold	200,000
Salary Expenses	45,000
Other Expenses	8,400

(19) Closing the Income Summary to Retained Earning account.

Dr. Income Summary 26,850

Cr. Retained Earnings 26,850

(20) Assume the tax is levied at 20%, so that the entry is:

Dr. Retained Earnings 5, 370

Cr. Income Tax Payable 5, 370

3.7 Preparing the Financial Statements

After the previous preparations, we can now start finishing the financial statements.

Financial statements are formal records of the financial activities and position of a business, person, or other entity. They are the final products of the accounting process, providing a report of the financial position of a unit.

Those who are interested in one entity may not be able to discover all the accounting data, and relevant financial information is presented in a structured manner and in a form which is easy to understand. That's why they would rely on a few statements and reports to have a clear understanding of the entity.

The basic financial statements include:

- Statement of financial position
- Statement of profit and loss and other comprehensive income
- Statement of cash flow
- Statement of owner's equity

We will focus on two sheets of financial statements in this chapter, namely, the statement of financial position, and statement of profit or loss.

3.7.1 The Statement of Financial Position

The statement of financial position, also known as balance sheet, reports a company's financial position (condition) at a given point in time, so that it is now called the statement of financial position.

The statement of financial position lists all assets, liabilities and

statement of financial position or balance sheet 资产负债表，作为时点报表，反映的是企业在某一时点的资产负债及权益情况。

statement of cash flow 现金流量表

statement of owner's equity 股东权益变动表

at a given point in time 在具体某个时点

tangible or intangible 有形的或无形的

account receivable 应收账款

owner's equity as of a business entity.

Assets can either be tangible or intangible. Examples of tangible assets include cash, account receivables, merchandise inventory, plants, equipments, buildings and machines. Trademarks, patents and copyrights are examples of intangible assets.

Liabilities are probable future sacrifices of economic benefits arising from the present obligations of a particular entity to transfer assets or provide services to other entities in the future as a result of past transactions or events. Accounts payable, notes payable, salaries payable, taxes payable, interests payable and bonds payable are typical examples of liabilities.

Owner's equity is a residual amount. The IASB's Framework defines equity as follows:

Equity is the residual interest in the assets that remains after deducting its liabilities. In a business enterprise, the entity is the ownership interest.

The statement of financial position shows that assets equal the sum of liabilities and owner's equity as the following equation:

Assets = Liabilities + Owner's Equity

Let's consider this equation in a different way. When a company is to start a business, we take a manufacturing company as an example, it requires the plant, machines and equipments to make products that can be traded in the market in order to generate profits for the company. The question is what the source of the assets is or how we can finance the assets. In other words, where do we get the money to acquire the assets we need?

In fact, assets can be financed by either liabilities or owner's equity. For instance, if a company plans to purchase a machine priced at \$20,000, \$10,000 can be financed by borrowing from the bank while the other \$10,000 can be financed by issuing shares to the owners. By borrowing from the bank and issuing shares to the owners, the company is capable of raising enough money to buy the machine.

merchandise inventory 商品存货

plant, equipment 厂房设备

trademark 商标

patent 专利

copyright 版权

accounts payable 应付账款

notes payable 应付票据

taxes payable 应交税费

interests payable 应付利息

bonds payable 应付债券

statement of profit and loss 利润表，作为时期报表，反映的是某一时间段内企业的经营情况，即是否盈利或亏损。

performance of a company 一个公司的业绩

3.7.2 Statement of Profit or Loss

The performance of a company is reported in the statement of profit or loss and other comprehensive income. IAS1, Presentation of Financial Statements, defines profit or loss as "the total of income less expenses, excluding the components of other comprehensive income". Other comprehensive income (OCI) is defined as comprising "items of income and expense (including reclassification adjustments) that are not recognized in profit or loss as required or permitted by other International Financial Reporting Standards (IFRS)". Total comprehensive income is defined as "the change in equity during a period resulting from transactions and other events, other than those changes resulting from transactions with owners in their capacity as owners".

Continue with the last example of Millie Company. We can prepare the statement of profit and loss and the statement of financial position as follow:

STATEMENT OF PROFIT AND LOSS FOR THE YEAR ENDED 31 DEC. 2015

unit: $

Sales		280, 000
Less: Cost of Goods Sold		
Purchase	200, 000	
Beginning Inventory	0	
Ending Inventory	0	(200, 000)
Gross Profits on Sales		80, 000
Operating Expenses:		
Salary Expenses	45, 000	
Depreciation Expenses	0	
Other Expenses	8, 400	(53, 400)
Total		26, 600
Operating Income		
Other Income:		

other comprehensive income (OCI) 其他综合收益

International Financial Reporting Standards (IFRS) 国际财务报告准则

(Continued)

Interest Income	150	
Rent Income	100	(250)
Net Income Before Tax		26, 850
Income Tax Payable		(5, 370)
Net Income After Tax		21, 480

STATEMENT OF FINANCIAL POSITION ON 31 DEC. 2015

unit: $

Assets		
Cash		35, 000
Note Receivable		50, 000
Accounts Receivable		30, 000
Interests Receivable		150
Prepaid Rent		4, 600
Office Equipment		30, 000
Less: Acc. Dep.		
Land		50, 000
Total Assets		199, 750
Liabilities		
Income Tax Payable		5, 370
Salary Payable		3, 000
Unearned Rent Income		100
Total Liabilities		8, 470
Owners'Equity		
Capital Stock		170, 000
Retained Earnings		21, 280
Total Liabilities and Owners' Equity		199, 750

Exercise 3

1. Entries making

Identify in each transaction which account should be debited and which one should be credited, to report to George's business.

(1) Mr. Lloyd introduces $50, 000 cash into the business.

(2) A machine costing $20, 000 cash.

(3) Goods for resale are bought for $3,500 on credit from Kevin.

(4) Goods for resale are bought and paid immediately for $4,000.

(5) $3,500 payable to Kevin is paid in cash.

(6) Part of the goods with book value of $3,000, are sold for $3,600 in cash.

(7) Wages of $1,000 are paid in cash.

2. Case.

The trial balance of Cooper on March 1st, 2019 lists the business's assets, liabilities and owners' equity on that date.

unit: $

Trial Balance as at March 1st		
	Debit	Credit
Cash	27,000	
Accounts receivable	4,500	
Accounts payable		2,000
Common stock		10,500
Retained earnings		19,000
	31,500	31,500

During March, the business completed the following transactions:

(1) Borrowed $45,000 from the bank.

(2) Paid cash of $40,000 to a real estate company to acquire land.

(3) Made service for a customer and received $5,000 in cash.

(4) Purchased supplies on credit, $2,000.

(5) Performed customer service and earned revenue on account for $2,600.

(6) Paid $1,200 on account for inventory.

(7) Paid the following cash expenses: salaries, $3,000; rent, $1,500; and interests, $400.

(8) Received $3,100 on account.

(9) Received a $200 utility bill that will be paid next week.

(10) Paid dividend of $1,800.

Requirement:

1) Journalize the preceding transactions.

2) Prepare the trial balance of the business on March 31st, 2019.

Chapter 4 Assets

In a company, there are some necessary resources that are used for the general operation, for example, cash, materials, goods for sold, computer, office buildings, equipment and so on.

resource 资源

In this chapter, we are going to talk about these resources in a company.

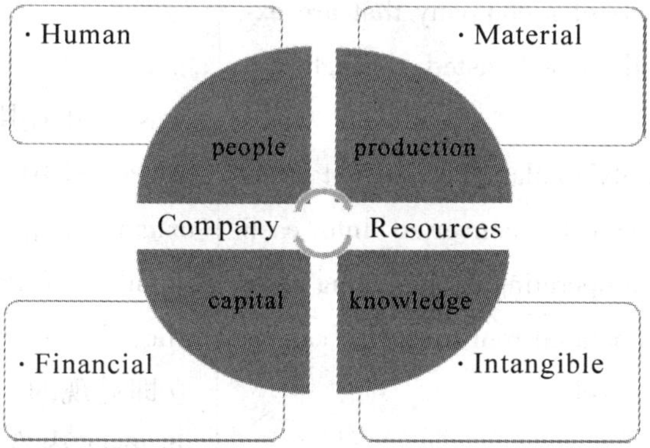

What else resources can you imagine that are useful and necessary for a company? And what are the intentions to hold those resources for a company?

Learning Objectives

After studying this chapter, you should understand and be able to:

▶ Explain the definition of asset.

▶ Explain what is included in the cash and cash equivalents amount reported on the balance sheet.

▶ Discuss how short-term marketable securities are reported on the balance sheet.

▶ Explain how inventories are reported on the balance sheet.

▶ Explain the difference of current and non-current assets.

▶ Explain what depreciation is, and the accounting treatment for depreciation.

In Chapter 2, we have learnt the definition of asset. Assets refer to resources owned and controlled by the entity as a result of past transactions and events, from which future economic benefits are expected to flow into the entity. We are going to study assets in detail in this chapter.

4.1 Current Assets

Current assets represent all the assets of a company that are expected to be sold, consumed, utilized or exhausted through the standard business operations.

A current asset is an item on an entity's balance sheet that is either cash, cash equivalent, or what can be converted into cash within one year. If an organization has an operating cycle lasting more than one year, an asset is still classified as a current asset if it can be converted into cash within one operating cycle.

Examples of current assets are:

√ Cash and cash equivalent

√ Accounts receivable

√ Inventory

√ Prepaid expenses

These items are typically presented in the balance sheet in their order of liquidity, which means that the most liquid items are shown at first.

Liquidity describes the degree to which an asset or security can

consumed 耗用，消费
utilized 使用
exhausted 用尽
liquidity 流动性
illiquid（资产）不可立即兑现的
intrinsic 内在的，真实的
convert 转换
collection 收藏品

be quickly bought or sold in the market at a price reflecting its intrinsic value, in other words, the ease of converting it to cash.

For example, if a person wants a $1,000 equipment, cash is the asset that can most easily be used to obtain it. If that person has no cash but a rare book collection that has been appraised at $1,000, he or she is unlikely to find someone willing to trade them the equipment for the collection. Instead, he or she will have to sell the collection and use the cash to purchase the equipment.

That may be fine if the person can wait for months or years to make the purchase, but it could present a problem if the person only had a few days. He/She may have to sell the book collection at a discount, instead of waiting for a buyer who is willing to pay the full value. Rare book collection is an example of an illiquid asset.

4.1.1 Cash and Cash Equivalents (CCE)

All companies need cash to run their business. They need to pay salaries to employees and bills, and to run their day-to-day operations.

cash and cash equivalents (CCE) 现金及现金等价物

When a company is not using its cash balance it may invest its cash in very low risk liquid (easily sold) securities so it can generate interest income.

Very liquid securities are sometimes called cash equivalents.

What Are Cash and Cash Equivalents (CCE)?

Cash and cash equivalents refers to the line item on the balance sheet that reports the value of a company's assets that are cash or can be converted into cash immediately. These include bank accounts, marketable securities, commercial paper, and short-term government bonds with a maturity date within three months or less.

Cash includes money on hand in change funds, petty cash, funds, and any funds immediately available to the firm in its bank accounts.

bank account 银行账户

marketable securities 有价证券

Cash equivalents are short-term investments readily convertible into cash with a minimal risk of price chance due to interest rate

commercial paper 商业票据

movements.

Can you find Cash and Cash Equivalent in the following balance sheet?

Balance sheet unit: $

Period Ending	30 Sep 2019
Asset	
Current Assets	
Cash and Cash Equivalents	13, 844, 000
Short-Term Investment	11, 233, 000
Receivables	31, 909, 000
Inventory	2, 100, 200
Other Current Assets	980, 900
Total Current Asset	60, 067, 100

Internal Control Over Cash

Since cash is the most liquid of all assets, a business cannot survive and prosper if it does not have adequate control over its cash.

Cash is the asset that has the greatest chance of "going missing" and that is why we must ensure that we have strong internal controls built around the cash process.

Since many business transactions involve cash, it is a vital factor in the operation of a business. Of all the company's assets, cash is the most easily mishandled either through theft or carelessness.

To control and manage its cash, a company should:

· Account for all cash transactions accurately so that correct information is available regarding cash flows and balances.

· Make certain that enough cash is available to pay bills as they come due.

· Avoid holding too much idle cash because excess cash could be invested to generate income, such as interest.

· Prevent loss of cash due to theft or fraud.

short-term government bonds 短期政府债券
petty cash 备用金
convertible 可转换的

internal control 内部控制
vital factor 关键因素

mishandled 处理不当
theft 盗窃
fraud 失误，错误
come due 到期
idle cash 闲置资金
going missing 丢失

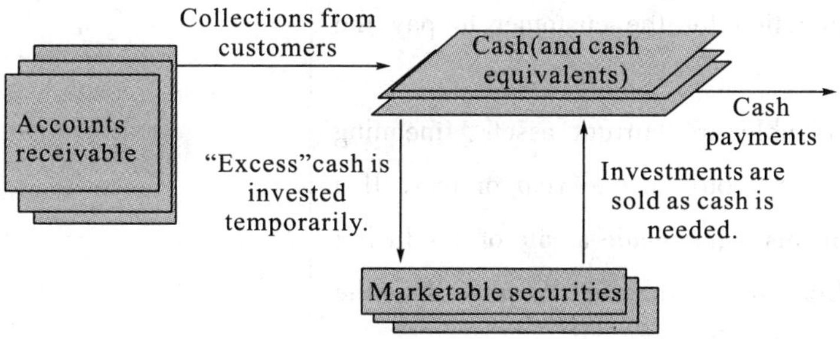

In the cash process, a company may keep appropriate amount of cash in order to pay its bills. Sometimes the company may not receive cash from customers due to trade credit. After the collection of cash from customers, the cash and cash equivalents will be increased. The financial manager in the company may decide which level of amount should be kept for the safety of operation. Idle cash, or "excess" cash can be then invested temporarily for interest income by buying marketable securities. When cash is needed, marketable securities are sold to convert cash.

4.1.2 Accounts Receivable

What Do Accounts Receivable Mean?

Accounts receivable are the balance of money due to a firm for goods or services delivered or used but not yet paid for by customers. Said another way, accounts receivable are amounts of money owed by customers to another entity for goods or services delivered or used on credit but not yet paid for by clients.

Accounts receivable refer to the outstanding invoices a company has or the money clients owe the company. The phrase refers to accounts a business has a right to receive because it has delivered a product or service.

Accounts receivable, or receivables represent a line of credit extended by a company and normally have terms that require payments due within a relatively short time period, ranging from a few days to a fiscal or calendar year.

Companies record accounts receivable as assets on their balance

account receivable 应收账款
outstanding 未支付的
credit 信用
fiscal 财政的
calendar 日历
legal obligation 法定义务
debtor 债务人
sale on credit 赊销
I owe you, IOU 欠条

sheets since there is a legal obligation for the customer to pay the debt.

Furthermore, accounts receivable are current assets, meaning the account balance is due from the debtor in one year or less. If a company has receivables, this means it has made a sale on credit but has yet to collect the money from the purchaser. Essentially, the company has accepted a short-term IOU from its client.

How Do Businesses Have Accounts Receivable?

Most companies operate by allowing a portion of their sales to be on credit. Sometimes, businesses offer this credit to frequent or special customers and receive periodic invoices.

The practice allows customers to avoid the hassle of physically making payments as each transaction occurs.

In other cases, businesses routinely offer all their clients the ability to pay after receiving the service.

For example, electric companies typically bill their clients after the clients have received the electricity.

While the electricity company waits for its customers to pay their bills, the company considers unpaid invoices a part of its accounts receivable.

Importance of Accounts Receivable

Accounts receivable are an important aspect of a business's fundamental analysis.

Accounts receivable are current assets so they are a measure of a company's liquidity or ability to cover short-term obligations without additional cash flows.

Fundamental analysts often evaluate accounts receivable in the context of turnover, which they call accounts receivable turnover ratio, and which measures the number of times a company has collected on its accounts receivable balance during an accounting period.

Further analysis would include days sales outstanding analysis, which measures the average collection period for a firm's receivables balance over a specified period.

fundamental analysis 基本面分析
turnover 周转率
collection period 赊销货款回收期
widget 小部件，小机械

Accounts Receivable Example

Let's assume that Company XYZ sells $1 million of widget parts to a widget manufacturer and gives that customer 60 days to pay for those parts.

In this case, once Company XYZ receives the order and/or sends the parts and/or sends the customer an invoice; it will increase sales revenue by $1 million and its accounts receivable by $1 million. When 60 days has passed and Company XYZ is paid, it will increase cash by $1 million and reduce its accounts receivable by $1 million.

Accounting Entries:

Dr. Accounts Receivable	1,000,000	
Cr. Sales Revenue		1,000,000
Dr. Cash	1,000,000	
Cr. Accounts Receivable		1,000,000

Accounts receivable is an asset, and as such, it appears on the balance sheet. In particular, accounts receivable are a current asset, meaning that the amount owed is expected to be received within the next 12 months or within one operating cycle.

Why Do Accounts Receivable Matter?

Accounts receivable are an important factor in a company's working capital.

If it's too high, the company may be lax in collecting what's owed to it and may soon be struggling to find the cash to pay the bills.

If it's too low, the company may be unwisely harming customer relationships or not offering competitive payment terms.

4.1.3 Inventory

What is inventory?

Inventory, often called merchandise, refers to goods and materials that a business holds for sale and raw materials used to produce goods available for sale in a near future.

They are not used in the process of producing things or promoting the business. The sole purpose of these current assets is to sell them

inventory 存货
merchandise 商品，货物
goods 商品
materials 材料

to customers for a profit, but an asset for sale doesn't mean that it's considered inventory.

We need to look at three main characteristics of inventory to determine whether an asset should be accounted for as merchandise.

First, the assets must be part of the company's primary business.

For instance, a sandwich shop's delivery truck is not considered inventory because it has nothing to do with the primary business of making and selling sandwiches. This is considered a fixed asset for the sandwich shop. To a car dealership, on the other hand, this truck would be considered inventory because it is in the business of selling vehicles.

Second, the assets must be available for sale or will soon be ready to sell.

If some business assets could be sold but are never actually made available for sale, they aren't inventory. These are just assets or investments of the company.

Third, the purpose of owning the assets must be to sell them to customers.

Going back to our sandwich shop example, the truck was never meant to be sold to a customer. It was purchased to deliver sandwiches and was sold when it couldn't perform that job. The car dealership, on the other hand, purchases vehicles for the sole purpose of reselling them. Thus, the truck is considered inventory to them.

Types of Inventory

According to our inventory definition, there are many different types of inventory and each is accounted for slightly differently.

Retailers are the easiest to account for because they typically only have one kind of goods called merchandise. They purchase inventory from wholesalers or manufacturers as finished products to sell to their customers.

Manufacturers, on the other hand, define inventory a little bit differently because they produce their own products to sell to customers. Thus, they need to account for the inventory at every stage of production.

retailer 零售商
wholesaler 批发商
category 种类，类别
raw material 原材料
work-in-process WIP 在产品
finished goods 产成品
partially finished product 半成品
survival 生存

The three categories are raw materials, work-in-process, and finished goods. Let's have a look at each of these categories in the Ford car plant.

Raw materials are the building blocks to make finished goods.

Ford purchases sheet metal, steel bars, and tubing to manufacture car frames and other parts. When they put these materials into produce and start cutting the bars and shaping the metal, the raw materials become work-in-process inventories.

Work-in-process inventory consists of all partially finished products that a manufacturer produces. As the unfinished cars make their way down the assembly line, they are considered a work-in-progress until they are finished.

Finished goods are exactly what they sound like. These are the finished products that can be sold to wholesalers, retailers, or even the end users. In Ford's case, they are finished cars that are ready to be sent to dealers.

Each of these different categories is important and managing them is key to any business's survival.

Inventory control is one of the most important concepts for any business especially retailers.

Since they purchase goods from manufacturers and resell them to consumers at small margins, they have to manage their purchasing and control the amount of cash that is tied up in merchandise.

inventory control 存货控制

margin 边际利润

Inventory Components and Cash Flow for a Typical Manufacturing Company:

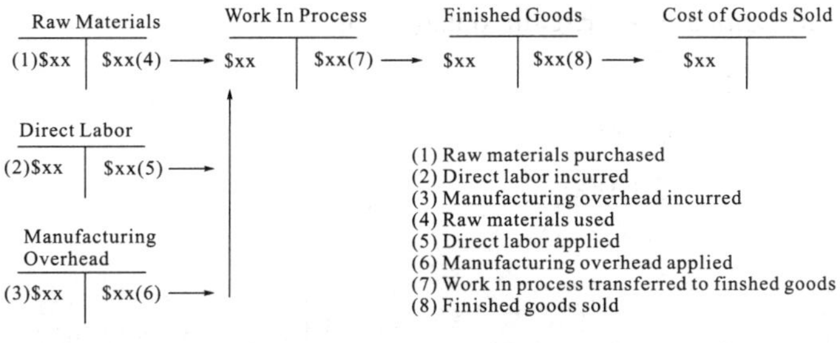

manufacturing company 制造型企业

direct labor 直接人工

manufacturing overhead 制造费用（间接成本）

cost of goods sold 销售成本

Related accounting treatment entries:

(1) Dr. Raw Material ××

Cr. Cash / Accounts Payable ××

(2) Dr. Direct Labor ××

Cr. Cash / Salary Payable ××

(3) Dr. Manufacturing Overhead ××

Cr. Cash / Accounts Payable ××

(4) Dr. Work in Process ××

Cr. Raw Material ××

(5) Dr. Work in Process ××

Cr. Direct Labor ××

(6) Dr. Work in Process ××

Cr. Manufacturing Overhead ××

(7) Dr. Finished Goods ××

Cr. Work in Process ××

(8) Dr. Cost of Goods Sold ××

Cr. Finished Goods ××

Examples for accounting treatment of inventory:

On Sep. 1, Company ABC purchased raw material by cash, amounting $ 10,000.

Dr. Inventory-Raw Material 10,000

Cr. Cash 10,000

On Sep. 5, Company ABC purchased merchandise D from Company EVER on account with the amount of $ 50,000, which will be due in 20 days.

Dr. Inventory-Merchandise D 50,000

Cr. Accounts Payable 50,000

On Sep. 20 Company ABC paid Company EVER the outstanding invoice.

Dr. Accounts Payable 50,000

Cr. Cash on Bank 50,000

purchase on account 赊购

account payable 应付账款

be due 到期

4.1.4 Prepaid Expenses

What Are Prepaid Expenses?

Prepaid expenses in accounting are those expenses which are to be incurred in future but the amount for the same has already been paid in advance.

Think of it as expenditure paid in one accounting period, but for which the related asset will not be consumed until a future period.

Take the example of Starbucks. The prepaid expense has been increasing since 2010. Starbucks paid cash for buying materials, for some services that should be used in the future.

Other Examples of Prepaid Expense

Suppose Company A has purchased Consulting Services from Company B and makes the payment for the fees for the same (\$1,000) per year in the next 5 years.

In this case, Company A will show (\$1,000) as yearly Expense and (\$4,000) would be shown in the Asset side of the Balance sheet as "Prepaid Expense" which subsequently be recorded as Expenditure every year for the next 4 years.

The accounting treatment for the prepaid expense is as follows:

Dr. Prepaid Expense	5,000	
Cr. Cash		5,000
Dr. Administrative Expense	1,000	
Cr. Prepaid Expense		1,000

prepaid expense 预付款项
pay in advance 预付
subsequent 后续的
administrative expense 管理费用

4.2 Non-current Assets

Assets can be divided into two categories: current and non-current.

As we have discussed before, current assets are items listed on a company's balance sheet that are expected to be converted into cash within one fiscal year.

Conversely, non-current assets are long-term assets that a company expects to hold over one fiscal year and cannot readily be converted into cash.

Current and non-current assets are located on the balance sheet. Non-current assets are a company's long-term investments or

non-current asset 非流动资产
fiscal year 财政年度
long-term investment 长期投资
intellectual property 知识产权
property, plant and equipment (PPE) 固定

long-term assets that have a useful life of more than one year.

Non-current assets cannot be easily converted to cash. Examples of non-current assets include long-term investments in other companies, intellectual property (e. g. patents), and property, plant and equipment.

资产（财产、厂房和设备）

notes receivable 应收票据

stock 股票

bond 债券

4. 2. 1 Long-Term Investments

Long-term investments are non-current assets that are not used in operating activities to generate revenues.

In other words, long-term investments are assets that are held for more than one year or accounting period and are used to create other income outside of the normal operations of the company.

Notes receivable, stocks, and bonds are typically considered to be long-term investments if management plans to keep them for more than one year.

None of these assets are traditionally used in operating activities.

For example, a company doesn't typically purchase bonds as part of its operations unless it's an investment firm.

4. 2. 2 Land & Building

Land is a long-term asset account that reports the cost of real property exclusive of the cost of any constructed assets on the property.

Land usually appears as the first item under the balance sheet heading of Property, Plant and Equipment.

Generally, land is not depreciated. Why?

The land asset is not depreciated, because it is considered to have an infinite useful life. This makes land unique among all asset types; it is the only one for which depreciation is prohibited.

Nearly all fixed assets have a useful life, after which they no longer contribute to the operations of a company or they stop generating revenue. During this useful life, they are depreciated, which reduces their cost to what they are supposed to be worth at the end of their useful lives.

Land, however, has no definitive useful life, so there is no

exclusive 独有的；除开的

constructed 建造的

depreciate *v.* 折旧

depreciation *n.* 折旧

infinite 无限的

prohibit 禁止

fixed assets 固定资产

no longer 不再

contribute to 贡献

useful life 使用年限

way to depreciate it. Instead, in the absence of natural resources that are to be extracted, land is considered to have an unlimited life span. Further, due to the scarcity of land, its value tends to increase over time, as opposed to the decline in value of most other types of fixed assets.

Buildings, however, should be depreciated according to its estimated useful life.

A company depreciates a building for financial reporting purposes at the end of an accounting period to account for the use of the building in its operations.

Depreciation reduces a building's value over its useful life on your small business's balance sheet and reduces your net income as an expense on your income statement.

4.2.3 Property, Plant, and Equipment

Property, Plant, and Equipment (PP&E) is a non-current, tangible capital asset shown on the balance sheet of a business and used to generate revenues and profits.

PP&E plays a key part in the financial planning and analysis of a company's operations and future expenditures, especially with regards to capital expenditures.

Extracts of Balance Sheet:

Balance Sheet
Assets
Cash
Accounts Receivable
Inventory
Current Assets
Property & Equipment
Goodwill
Non-current Assets
Total Assets

The PP&E account is often denoted as net of accumulated depreciation.

This means that if a company does not purchase additional new

definitive 明确的，最后的
scarcity 稀缺
estimated 估计的，预测的
tangible 有形的
expenditure 支出
capital expenditure 资本化支出
accumulated depreciation 累计折旧
stock shares 股票
identifiable 可识别的，可辨认的

equipment, then Net PP&E should slowly decrease in value every year due to depreciation. This can be better determined by a depreciation schedule.

PP&E is a fixed-asset account item and is generally very illiquid. A company can sell its equipment, but not as easily as it can sell its inventory or investments such as bonds or stock shares.

The value of PP&E between companies will vary with the operations.

For example, a construction company will generally have a significantly higher property, plant, and equipment balance than an accounting firm does.

PP&E assets are tangible, identifiable, and expected to generate an economic return for the company for more than one year or one operating cycle (whichever is longer).

The account can include machinery, equipment, vehicles, buildings, land, office space, office equipment, and furnishings, among other things.

Note that, of all these asset classes, land is generally one of the only assets that do not typically depreciate over time.

PP&E Formula

Net PP&E = Gross PP&E + Capital Expenditures-Accumulated Depreciation

Example

In May 2019, Factory Corp. owned PP&E machinery with a gross value of $ 5,000,000.

Accumulated depreciation for the same machinery was at $ 2,100,000.

Due to the wear and tear of the machinery, the company decided to purchase another $ 1,000,000 in new equipment.

For this period, the depreciation expense for all old and new equipment is $ 150,000.

Thus, the ending balance is $ 3,750,000.

This is found by taking $ 5,000,000 + $ 1,000,000 −

gross value 总值

wear and tear 日久耗损

probable 很有可能

future economic benefits 未来经济利益

measured reliably 可以可靠计量

initial costs 初始成本

$ 2, 100, 000 - $ 150, 000.

Recognition and Measurement of PP&E

PP&E should be recognized by a company only if:

It is probable that future economic benefits associated with the asset will flow to the entity over a period of more than one year; and the cost of the asset can be measured reliably.

The initial costs of a PP&E item may include:

Its purchase price, any import duties, non-refundable taxes, sales discounts, and rebates;

Any costs directly attributable to bringing the asset to the location and condition necessary for it to be operational;

And an estimated value of the costs of dismantling and removing the asset and restoring the site on which it is located. This is commonly referred to as an asset retirement obligation (ARO).

Depreciation of PP&E

The other major component of the PP&E formula above is depreciation and amortization.

Depreciation reduces the value of property, plant, and equipment on the balance sheet as the value of assets is lowered over time due to wear and tear and the reduction of their useful life.

The depreciation expense is used to reduce the value of the net balance and it flows to the income statement as an expense.

The main types of depreciation methods are as follows:

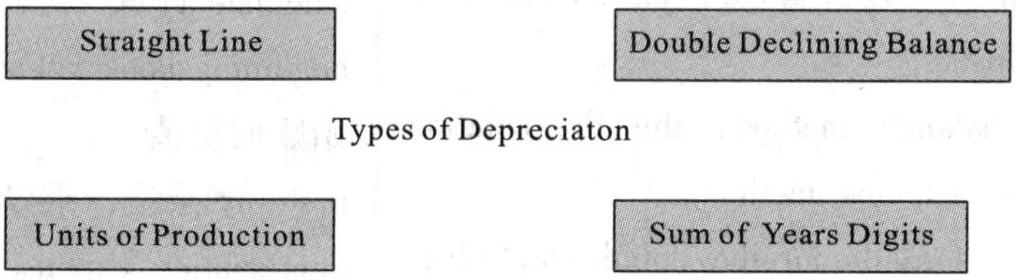

1) Straight-Line Depreciation Method

Straight-line depreciation is a very common, and the simplest method of calculating depreciation expense. In straight-line depreciation, the expense amount is the same every year over the useful life of the asset.

purchase price 采购价

import duties 进口关税

non-refundable taxes 不可退还的税额

sales discounts 销售折扣

rebates 退还（部分付款）

dismantling 拆卸（机器）

asset retirement obligation (ARO) 资产弃置义务，也叫弃置成本，指根据国家法律和行政法规、国际公约等规定，企业承担的环境保护和生态恢复等义务所确定的支出。

straight-line depreciation 直线法折旧

sum of the years' digits 年限总和法

units of production 工作量法

double declining balance 双倍余额递减法

depreciation formula 折

The following is depreciation formula for the Straight-Line Method:

Depreciation Expense = (Cost-Salvage Value) / Useful Life

Example

Consider a piece of equipment that costs $25,000 with an estimated useful life of 8 years and a $0 salvage value. The depreciation expense per year for this equipment would be as follows:

Depreciation Expense = ($25,000-$0) / 8 = $3,125 per year

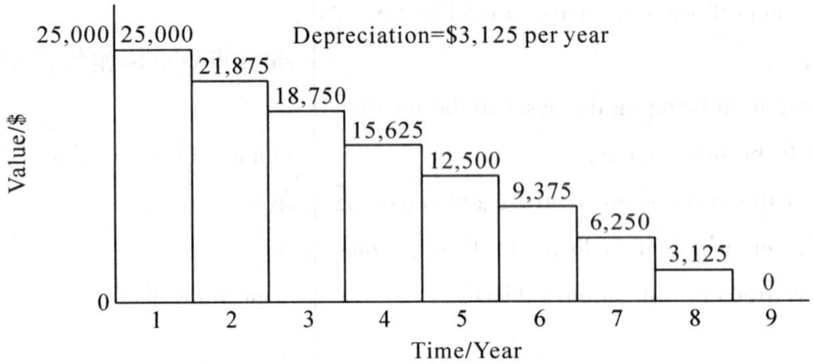

Straight Line Depreciation

2) Double Declining Balance Depreciation Method

Compared to other depreciation methods, double-declining-balance depreciation results in a larger amount expensed in the earlier years as opposed to the later years of an asset's useful life.

The method reflects the fact that assets are typically more productive in their early years than in their later years, and also, the practical fact that any asset (think of buying a car) loses more of its value in the first few years of its use.

With the double-declining-balance method, the depreciation factor is 2 times of the straight-line expense method.

The following is depreciation formula for the double-declining-balance method:

Periodic Depreciation Expense = Beginning book value × Rate of depreciation

Example

Consider a piece of property, plant, and equipment (PP&E)

旧计算公式
salvage value 残值
useful life 使用年限

rate of depreciation 折旧率
calculate 计算
beginning book value 初始账面价值
multiply 乘法，乘以
depreciation expense 折旧费用
subtract 扣除
ending book value 期末账面价值

that costs $ 250, 000, with an estimated useful life of 8 years and a $ 2, 500 salvage value. To calculate the double-declining-balance depreciation, We set up a schedule:

The information on the schedule is explained below:

The beginning book value of the asset is filled in at the beginning of year 1 and the salvage value is filled in at the end of year 8.

The rate of depreciation (Rate) is calculated as follows:

Rate of depreciation = (100% / Useful life of asset)×2

= (100% / 8)×2 = 25%

Note: Since this is a double-declining method, we multiply the rate of depreciation by 2.

Multiply the rate of depreciation by the beginning book value to determine the expense for that year. For example, $ 25, 000×25% = $ 6, 250 depreciation expense.

Subtract the expense from the beginning book value to arrive at the ending book value. For example, $ 25, 000 − $ 6, 250 = $ 18, 750 ending book value at the end of the first year.

The ending book value for that year is the beginning book value for the following year. For example, the year 1 ending book value of $ 18, 750 would be the year 2 beginning book value. Repeat this until the last year of useful life.

sum-of-the-years'-digits method 年数总和法
remaining life 剩余年数
formula 公式
estimated 估计的，预计的
accelerated depreciation 加速折旧

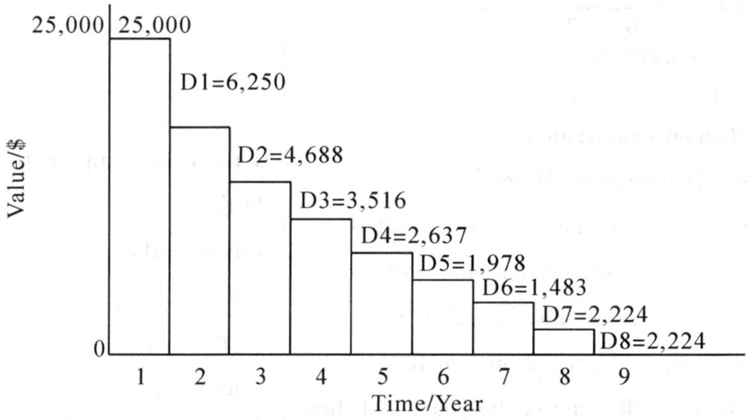

Note: D1 means depreciation for Year 1, and so on.

Double Declining Balance Depreciation

3) Units-of-Production Depreciation Method

The units-of-production depreciation method depreciates assets based on the total number of hours used or the total number of units to be produced by using the asset, over its useful life.

The following is the formula for the units-of-production method:

Depreciation Expense = (Number of units produced / Life in number of units) × (Cost−Salvage value)

Example

Consider a machine that costs \$25,000, with an estimated total unit production of 100 million and a \$0 salvage value. During the first quarter of activity, the machine produced 4 million units.

To calculate the depreciation expense using the formula above: Depreciation Expense = (4 million / 100 million) × (\$25,000−\$0) = \$1,000

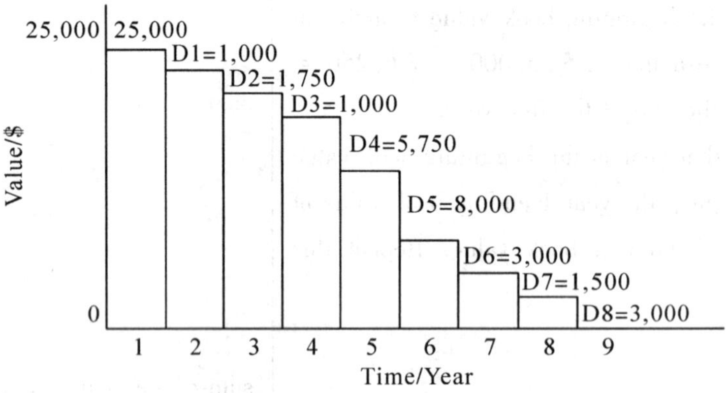

Note: D1 means depreciation for Year 1, and so on.

Units of Production Depreciation

4) Sum-of-the-Years'-Digits Depreciation Method

The sum-of-the-years'-digits method is one of the accelerated depreciation methods. A higher expense is incurred in the early years and a lower expense in the latter years of the asset's useful life.

In the sum-of-the-years'-digits depreciation method, the remaining life of an asset is divided by the sum of the years and then multiplied by the depreciating base to determine the depreciation expense.

a piece of equipment 一件设备
salvage value 残值
constant 固定不变的
at the beginning of the year 年初
multiply 相乘，乘以
a declining trend 减少的趋势

The following is the depreciation formula for the sum-of-the-years'-digits method:

Depreciation Expense = (Remaining life / Sum of the years digits) × (Cost−Salvage value)

Consider the following example to more easily understand the concept of the sum-of-the-years'-digits depreciation method.

Example

Consider a piece of equipment that costs $25,000 and has an estimated useful life of 8 years and a $0 salvage value. To calculate the sum-of-the-years'-digits depreciation, set up a schedule, and the information in the schedule is explained below:

1. The depreciation base is constant throughout the years and is calculated as follows:

Depreciation Base = Cost − Salvage value depreciation base = $25,000− $0= $25,000

2. The remaining life is simply the remaining life of the asset. For example, at the beginning of the year, the asset has a remaining life of 8 years. The following year, the asset has a remaining life of 7 years, etc.

3. RL / SYD is "remaining life divided by sum of the years." In this example, the asset has a useful life of 8 years. Therefore, the sum of the years would be 1 + 2 + 3 + 4 + 5 + 6 + 7 + 8 = 36 years. The remaining life in the beginning of Year 1 is 8. Therefore, the RM / SYD = 8 / 36 ≈ 0.222.

4. The RL / SYD number is multiplied by the depreciating base to determine the expense for that year.

5. The same is done for the following years. In the beginning of Year 2, RL / SYD would be 7 / 36 ≈ 0.194. 0.194 × $25,000 = $4,850 expense for Year 2.

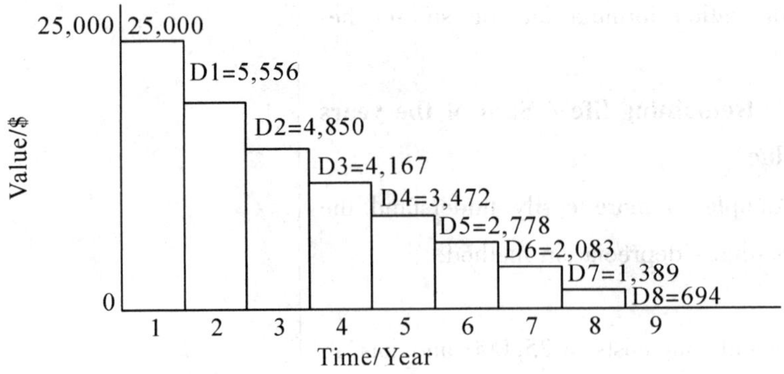

Note: D1 means depreciation for Year 1, and so on

Sum-of-the-Years Digits Depreciation

From the above calculation, we can observe that the depreciation expenses using sum-of-the-years' digits decrease from the first year to the end of the useful life, following a declining trend.

Can you find out a similar trend in the above mentioned depreciation method?

Think about the following question.

What is the economic impact for the declining trend of the depreciation?

Please keep in mind that, the remaining value of an asset is recoganized and reported in the balance sheet, or the statement of financial position.

However, the depreciation expenses will be reported in the income statement, or the statement of profit or loss. More deprecitaion expense in the first years will lead to less profit, and, the profit may experience an upward trend in the following year.

similar trend 相似的趋势
economic impact 经济影响
experience 经历
upward trend 向上增长的趋势

4.2.4 Intangibles

An intangible asset is an asset that lacks a physical substance.

Reputation, name recognition, and intellectual property such as knowledge and know-how.

Intangible assets are the long-term resources of an entity, which do not have physical existence.

intangible asset 无形资产
physical substance 实物
reputation 名声，名望
knowledge 知识
know-how 秘诀；专门技术

They derive their value from intellectual or legal rights, and from the value they add to the other assets.

Intangible assets are generally classified into two broad categories:

(1) definite life intangible assets, such as patents, copyrights, and goodwill, and

(2) infinite life intangible assets, such as trademarks.

In contrast to tangible assets, intangible assets cannot be destroyed by fire, hurricane, or other accidents or disasters and can help build back destroyed tangible assets.

How does it work?

Example

For example, goodwill, patents, trademarks and copyrights are intangible assets. None of these assets can be physically touched, but they can still have value.

The line item for intangible assets is found on the balance sheet. Though goodwill is considered an intangible asset, it's often listed as a separate line item.

Why does it matter?

Intangible assets can be a significant percentage of a company's total assets, and therefore have a big impact on a firm's book value.

In most cases, an analyst calculating book value will only include those intangible assets that can be separated from the company and sold.

Goodwill cannot be separated from the company, so it is generally not included in book value calculations. But a valuable patent can be sold and would be included in book value.

Three critical attributes of an intangible asset are:

√ identifiability

√ control (power to obtain benefits from the asset)

√ future economic benefits (such as revenues or reduced future costs)

How to calculate the amortization of intangible assets?

definite life intangible assets 固定寿命的无形资产
infinite life intangible assets 寿命不确定的无形资产
hurricane 飓风，暴风
disaster 灾难
goodwill 商誉
patent 专利
trademark 商标
copyright 版权

Accountants amortize intangible assets just like they depreciate physical capital assets.

What does amortization actually mean?

The process of amortization reduces the value of the intangible asset on the balance sheet over time and reports an expense on the income statement each period to reflect the change on the balance sheet during the given period.

Like depreciation, there are multiple methods a company can use to calculate an intangible asset's amortization, but the simplest is the straight-line method.

With the straight-line method, the company starts with the asset's recorded value, its residual value, and its useful life. The recorded value is the initial value assigned to the asset on the books, generally meaning its price or cost to create. Its residual value is the expected value of the asset at the end of its useful life.

For most intangible assets, the residual value is zero as many intangible assets are considered worthless once they've been fully utilized. The useful life of the asset is the period of time over which the company expects the intangible asset to provide economic value to the business.

Let's say that a company has developed a software solution to be used internally to better manage its inventory. The company does not intend to ever sell this software; it's only to be used by company staff.

This software is considered an intangible asset, and it must be amortized over its useful life.

First, the company will record the cost to create the software on its balance sheet as an intangible asset. The software cost the company \$12,000, in this case.

Next, the company estimates that the software will have a useful life of just three years given the fast-paced nature of software innovation.

At the end of three years, the company reckons that their internal software will have no remaining value, so its residual value is

be separated from 从……区别开来
attribute 特性，属性
identifiability 可识别性
control 控制
amortize 摊销
residual value 剩余价值；残值

therefore zero.

The company will use the straight-line method to report the amortization of the software, $ 4, 000 each year.

Exercise 4

1. Single choices.

(1) Which of the following is not a current asset?

A. Land and building

B. Inventory

C. Cash and cash equivalent

D. Accounts receivable

(2) Which of the following is not a non-current asset?

A. Patent

B. Goodwill

C. Long-term investment

D. Inventory

(3) Which of the following is not a depreciation method?

A. Straight-line method

B. Double-declining-balancing method

C. Sum-of-the-years'-digits method

D. Lower of cost and market value

(4) Which of the following is not included as inventory?

A. Raw materials

B. Work-in-process

C. Finished goods

D. Cost of goods sold

2. Please translate the following terms into Chinese.

(1) cash and cash equivalents

(2) inventory

(3) non-current asset

(4) property, plant and equipment

(5) intangible asset

(6) goodwill

（7） depreciation

（8） amortization

（9） balance

（10） marketable securities

（11） petty cash

（12） market value

（13） units-of-production depreciation

（14） wear and tear

（15） future economic benefit

3. Accounting treatment exercises.

1） Calculation.

A machine is purchased at the beginning of 2019 for \$36,000. Its estimated life is 6 years. Freight cost on the machine is \$2,000 and the installation costs are \$1,200. The machine is estimated to have a residual value of \$500 and a useful life of 40,000 hours. It was used 6,000 hours in 2019.

（1） What is the cost of the machine for accounting purpose?

（2） Calculate the depreciation charge for 2019 using the following method：

a） Straight-line-depreciation method

b） Units-of-production-depreciation method

2） Please write down the accounting entries.

（1） On Sep. 1 2019, Company ABC purchased raw materials at the price of \$5,000 by cash.

（2） On Sep. 5 2019, Company ABC applied raw materials amounting \$2,000 into the production line.

（3） On Sep. 10, Company ABC sold product at the price \$7,000 and the cost of goods related are \$3,000. (Revenue, Cost of goods sold)

（4） At the end of Sep. 2019, the depreciation of PPE is \$4,000, which is used in the production line. (Manufacturing overhead)

（5） On Sep. 20, Company ABC acquired an intangible asset at the market value of \$9,000 by cash.

（6） The amortization of intangible asset for Sep. 2019 is calculated as \$3,000.

4. Questions for review of key topics.

（1） What is the meaning of asset? Can you explain the major characteristics of asset in your own words?

(2) What is the definition of current asset? Can you name some kinds of current assets?

(3) Liquidity is important to understand the classification of current asset and non-current asset. What does liquidity mean in an economic environment?

(4) Inventory in a manufacturing company plays an important role in the business cycle. Can you explain the accounting process of production from raw materials to inventory?

(5) What is the intention of keeping cash and cash equivalent?

(6) What kind of company would have transactions of long-term investment?

(7) What is the meaning of depreciation? Please name the four regular depreciation methods.

Broaden your Perspective

What Is Just-in-Time (JIT)?

The just-in-time (JIT) inventory system is a management strategy that aligns raw-material orders from suppliers directly with production schedules. Companies employ this inventory strategy to increase efficiency and decrease waste by receiving goods only as they need them for the production process, which reduces inventory costs. This method requires producers to forecast demand accurately.

The JIT inventory system contrasts with just-in-case strategies, wherein producers hold sufficient inventories to have enough product to absorb maximum market demand.

One example of a JIT inventory system is a car manufacturer that operates with low inventory levels but heavily relies on its supply chain to deliver the parts it requires to build cars, on an as-needed basis. Consequently, the manufacturer orders the parts required to assemble the cars, only after an order is received.

For JIT manufacturing to succeed, companies must have steady production, high-quality workmanship, glitch-free plant machinery, and reliable suppliers.

JIT production systems cut inventory costs because manufacturers do not have to pay storage costs. Manufacturers are also not left with

Just-in-Time（JIT）准时生产，又译为实时生产系统，简称 JIT 系统，在 1953 年由日本丰田公司的副总裁大野耐一提出。其实质是保持物质流和信息流在生产中的同步，实现以恰当数量的物料，在恰当的时候进入恰当的地方，生产出恰当质量的产品。这种方法可以减少库存、缩短工时、降低成本、提高生产效率。

unwanted inventory if an order is canceled or not fulfilled.

Famous for its JIT inventory system, Toyota Motor Corporation orders parts only when it receives new car orders. Although the company installed this method in the 1970s, it took 15 years to perfect it.

Sadly, Toyota's JIT inventory system nearly caused the company to come to a screeching halt in February 1997, after a fire at Japanese-owned automotive parts supplier Aisin decimated its capacity to produce P-valves for Toyota's vehicles. Because Aisin is the sole supplier of this part, its weeks-long shut down caused Toyota to halt production for several days.

This caused a ripple effect, where other Toyota parts suppliers likewise had to temporarily shut down because the automaker had no need for their parts during that time period. Consequently, this fire cost Toyota 160 billion yen in revenue.

Chapter 5 Liabilities

Introduction

When you set up or run a firm, what are your general views on various sources of outside financing? Usually, firms may make use of various bank sources for both long-term and short-term loans. The majority of long-term outside financing come from borrowing long-term debt from the bank and issuing of bonds or debentures. Most of the short-term outside financing come from borrowing short-term debt from the bank and directly financing from suppliers.

sources of outside financing 外部融资来源

issue of bonds or debentures 发行债券

Both the above long-term and short-term debt are liabilities. However, how did the liabilities come into being? Naturally, to obtain the revenue, a business has to incur a certain amount of expenses. Assume an expense benefits the current period, but the actual payment for the expense will be made in a latter accounting period. Then as what we have learned the accrual basis accounting requires, the expense should be recorded in the current period. For instance, the company gets a 3-month loan of \$10,000 from the bank at the annual interest rate of 10%. Total of \$11,000 principal and interest won't be paid until three months later. Although \$1,000 of the interest expense is to be paid in a later period, it benefits the 3 months after the loan, so it should be apportioned over 3 months.

◎企业要获取一定的收入，自然就会产生一定的费用。如果一笔费用使当期产生收益，但这笔费用的实际支付却是在以后的某个会计期间，那么，按我们之前学的权责发生制的要求，这笔费用就应在本期记录。

annual interest rate 年利率

Learning Objective

After studying this chapter, you should understand and be

principal 本金

able to:

- Explain the definition of liability.
- Explain the typical accounting title of current liability.
- Discuss how sale tax pay on behalf of a company.
- Explain what bonds payable are.
- Explain how to treat bond issuing at par value and discount value.

interest 利息

apportion 分摊

5.1 Definition of Liability

A liability is a present obligation of the entity to transfer economic resources as a result of past events. An obligation is a duty of responsibility that the entity has no practical ability to avoid. Liabilities are generally classified into current liabilities and non-current liabilities.

current liability 流动负债

5.2 Definition of Current Liability

present obligation 现时义务

Current liabilities are present obligations that must be paid within one year or within its normal operating cycle. The typical current liabilities include accounts payable, notes payable, overdraft, current portion of long-term debt, unearned revenue, sale taxes payable and accrued expenses.

account payable 应付账款

5.2.1 Account Payable

Accounts payable are unpaid balance due to a creditor for products or services purchased on account. Usually accounts payable are divided into the categories of trade accounts payable and other accounts payable. Trade accounts payable are short-term obligations to suppliers for purchases or merchandise. Other accounts payable include liabilities for any goods and services other than merchandise.

Illustration 5. 1

Apple Company buys a machine for $65,000 on credit. What is the accounting entry of this transaction?

The explanation is as follows:

Apple Co. buys a machine, which will increase the asset. The increase of the asset should be recorded in the debit side. Apple Co. does not pay for the machine instead it pays later, which will increase the company's liability. The increase of liability should be recorded in the credit side. And we come to the accounting entry of the transaction:

Dr. Machine 65, 000

Cr. Accounts payable 65, 000

5. 2. 2 Notes Payable

Notes payable are written promises to pay stated sums of money at future date. Companies often issue short-term notes payable to borrow money from a bank or to purchase assets. Notes payable usually request the borrower to pay an interest charge. Under accounting treatment, the interest rate is stated separately from the principal amount of the note.

Illustration 5. 2

On 1 January, Apple Company borrows $80,000 from its bank for a period of eight months at an annual interest rate of 10%. Eight months later, Apple Co. will have to pay the bank the principal of $80,000 and the six months interest. As an evidence of this loan, the bank requires Apple Co. to issue a note payable. What are the accounting entries of this transaction?

The explanation is as follows:

The transaction is a process of borrowing, interest occurring and repayment of principal and interest. So the accounting entries are occurred in these three moment. At the date of borrowing, the cash and note payable are affected. During the six months, the interest should be recorded on interest expense and interest payable account.

categories 类别
short-term 短期的
obligation 义务
buy on credit 赊购
note payable 应付票据
written promise 书面承诺
principal 本金
annual interest rate 年利率

borrowing 借款
repayment 还款

Finally, when payment of the note, the note payable, interest payable and cash will be affected.

Now we come to the accounting entries of the transaction:

1 January-borrow the note

Dr. Cash	80,000	
Cr. Note payable		80,000

At the end of every month (from 1 Jan. - 30 Jun.) - record the interest

Dr. Interest expense	666.67	
Cr. Interest payable		666.67

At the date of repayment of principal and interest

Dr. Notes payable	80,000	
Interest expense	4,000	
Cr. Cash		84,000

interest 利息

interest expense 利息费用

interest payable 应付利息

unearned revenue 未实现的收入

deferred revenue 递延收益

5.2.3 Unearned Revenue

Unearned revenues are also called deferred revenues, which arise when a customer pays in advance. It indicates that the company has received money from its customers before earning the revenue. The company has an obligation to "pay" by rendering services or providing goods to the customer.

Illustration 5.3

Apple Company signed up a contract with Bee Company to perform services. Apple Co. received an advanced cash payment in the amount of $ 30,000 and the term of the contract was one month. The transaction acts to increase assets (cash) and liabilities (unearned revenue). One month later, Apple Co. performed the services for 30,000. What are accounting entries of the transaction?

The following is the explanation:

There are two transactions during these processes. The first transaction is Bee Company's payment in advance. This will increase Apple Co.'s asset and liability. Apple Co.'s performance of debit the cash and credit the unearned revenue. The second transaction is

Apple Co.'s performance of the service. This will decrease the liability and realize the revenue. Apple Co. should debit the unearned revenue and credit the revenue.

When receiving cash in advance:

Dr. Cash 30,000

Cr. Unearned revenue 30,000

When service is performed:

Dr. Unearned revenue 30,000

Cr. Revenue 30,000

5.2.4 Sales Tax Payable

Sales tax is an indirect tax levied on the sale of goods and services. It is usually administered by the local tax authorities.

Sales tax is a cumulative tax, collected at various stages during the life of goods or services. In the example below, a manufacturer of a mobile phone buys materials and components and then sells the mobile phone to a wholesaler, who in turn sells it to a retailer, who then sells it to a customer. It is assumed that the rate for sales tax is 13% on all items. All the other figures are for illustration only.

administer 管理
tax authority 税收征管部门
cumulative 累积的
components 零部件；零件
assume 假设

Illustration 5.4

unit: $

Stage	*Deseription*	*Price (net of sales tax)*	*Sales tax 13%*	*Total price*
Manufacture stage	Manufacturer purchases raw materials and components	100	13	113
	Manufacturer sells the completed television to a wholesaler	500	65	565
	Manufacturer hands over to tax authorities		52	
Wholesale stage	Wholesaler purchases the television	500	65	565
	Wholesaler sells the television to a retailer	800	104	904
	Wholesaler hands over to tax authorities		39	

(Continued)

Stage	*Deseription*	*Price (net of sales tax)*	*Sales tax 13%*	*Total price*
Retail stage	Retailer purchases the television	800	104	904
	Retailer sells the television	1,200	156	1,356
	Retailer hands over to tax authorities		52	
Ultimate customer	Customer purchases the television	1,200	156	1,356

The total tax of $156 is borne by the ultimate customer but is collected on behalf of the tax authorities at the different stages in the product's life. If we assume that the sales tax of $13 on the initial supplies to the manufacturer is paid by the supplier, the tax authorities would collect the sales tax as follows.

ultimate 最终的

accrued expense 应计费用

Stages	$
Supplies of materials and components	13
Manufacture	52
Wholesale	39
Retail	52
Total sales tax paid	156

Sales tax charged on sales is collected by the company on behalf of the tax authorities. So, sales tax does not form part of the revenue of the company.

The accounting treatment for sales tax payable is by debiting the cash, bank or receivable and by crediting sales tax payable.

For example, the retailer company sells the mobile phone for $1,200; the sales tax is $156. The total price is $1,356, and the sales account would only record the $1,200 excluding sales tax. The accounting entry to record this transaction would be as follows.

Dr. Bank 1,356

Cr. Sales revenue 1, 200

Sales tax payable 156

5. 2. 5 Accrued Expenses

Accrued expenses are expenses which relate to an accounting period but have not been paid for. According to the matching principal, the gross profit for a period should be calculated by matching sales and the cost of goods sold. In the same way, the profit for the year for a period should be calculated by charging the expenses which relate to that period. It includes an accrued interest on notes payable at the end of a period, accrued utility expenses and taxes, amortization of depreciation, accrued rent expenses and so on.

The accounting treatment for accrued expenses is by debiting expenses and crediting liability.

For example, the salary for the staffs in the retailer company for the month April is amounting $10, 000, however, the company usually pays its staff on May 5. The salary expense for April should be recognized, as the staff already worked in April and the company should recognize an operation expense, even though the cash payment happens in the next month. The accounting entry to record this transaction in April would be as follows.

Dr. Salary expenses 10, 000

Cr. Salary payable 10, 000

5. 2. 6 Contingent Liabilities

A contingent liability may be regarded as a possible liability, which may develop into a full-fledged liability or may be eliminated entirely by a future event.

endorse 背书

maturity 到期

contingent liability 或有负债

For example, when a business endorses a note and turns it over to a bank for cash, the business is contingently liable to the bank. If the note maker pays on the maturity date, the contingent liability of the endorser is thereby ended. But if the maker defaults, the endorser must pay in his instead. In either case, the period of the contingent liability ends at the maturity date of the note.

5.3 Non-current Liability

Large companies cannot borrow billions from a single lender because no one will risk that much money on a single company. How do large companies borrow huge amounts of money? They issue bonds to the public. Bonds payable are groups of notes payable issued to multiple lenders, called bondholders. In this part, we treat bonds payable and long-term notes payable together because their accounting is the same.

5.3.1 Definition of Non-current Liability

Non-current liabilities are present obligations that are not due within one year or a normal operating cycle. The typical non-current liabilities include bonds payable, long-term notes payable and mortgages payable. Because bonds are a common form of a long-term debt, they will be used to explain the key accounting procedures for long-term liabilities.

5.3.2 Bonds Payable

Introduction of Bond

To gain access to large amounts of cash, a company may issue bonds. Each bond is a long-term note payable that pays interest. Bonds payable are debts of the issuing company.

Purchases of bonds receive a bond certificate, which carries the issuing company's name. The certificate also states the principal, the amount that the company has borrowed from the bondholder. The face value (maturity value/par value) of a bond is $1,000. The issuing company pay the holder principal amount at a specific future data called the maturity data. The data also appears on the bond certificate.

non-current liability 非流动负债
bond 债券
note payable 应付票据
bondholder 债券持有者
within one year 一年之内
a normal operating cycle 一个正常的经营周期
mortgage payable 应付抵押贷款
interest 利息
certificate 有效凭证，权证
face value 票面价值
principal 本金
maturity date 到期日
market price 市场价值
present value 现值

Bondholders loan their money to companies for a price: interest on the principal. The bond certificate states the interest rate that the issuer will pay the holder and the dates that the interest payments are due. Generally, it is paid twice a year. When the company pays back the principal, the holder returns the certificate.

Bond Interest Rate

Bonds are sold at market price, which is the amount that investors are willing to pay at any given time. Market price is the bond's present value, which equals the present value of the principal payment plus the present value of the cash interest payments.

There are two interest rates. They work to set the price of a bond.

The contract interest rate, or stated interest rate, is the interest rate that determines the amount of cash interest the borrower pays and the investor receives each year. For example, CAA Corporation's 9% bonds have a contract interest rate of 9%. Thus, CAA pays \$9,000 of interest annually on each \$100,000 bond. Each semi-annual interest payment is \$4,500.

The market interest rate is the rate that investors demand for loaning their money. The market rate varies, and sometimes daily. A company may issue bonds with a contract interest rate that differs from the prevailing market interest rate. The following form shows how the contract interest rate and the market interest rate interact to determine the issuance price of a bond payable. CAA, for example, may issue its 9% bonds when the market rate has risen to 10%. Will the CAA bonds attract investors in this market? No, because investors can earn 10% on other bonds of similar risk. Therefore, investors will purchase CAA bonds only at a price less than par value. The difference between the lower price and face value is a discount. Conversely, if the market interest rate is 8%, CAA's 9% bonds will be so attractive that investors will pay more than face value for them. The difference between the higher price and face value is premium.

determine 决定
semi-annual 半年的
issuance price 发行价格
conversely 相反地
par value 票面价值
discount 折价
premium 溢价

Par value (9%)	Discount (8%)	Premium (10%)
Contract interest rate = Market interest rate	Contract interest rate < Market interest rate	Contract interest rate > Market interest rate
$ 1,000 bond issued for $ 1,000	$ 1,000 bond issued below $ 1,000	$ 1,000 bond issued above $ 1,000

Illustration 5.5: Bond issue at par value

Assume that CAA Company plans to issue $ 1,000,000 face value of 10%, 10-year bonds. At the issuance date of June 1, the going market rate of interest is 10%. CAA sells at the par value. The issuance of the bonds will be recorded by the following double entry:

Dr. Cash 1,000,000

Cr. Bonds payable 1,000,000

Illustration 5.6: Bond issue at discount

Assume that CAA Company plans to issue $ 1,000,000 face value of 10%, 10-year bonds. At the issuance date of June 1, the going market rate of interest is slightly above 10%. CAA sells at a market value of only $ 950. The issuance of the bonds will be recorded by the following double entry:

Dr. Cash 950,000

Discount on bonds payable 50,000

Cr. Bonds payable 1,000,000

Exercise 5

1. Please translate the following terms into Chinese.

(1) current liability

(2) overdraft

(3) notes payable

(4) account payable

(5) other payable

(6) unearned revenue

(7) accrued wages

(8) dividends payable

(9) corporation tax payable

(10) sales tax

(11) income tax payable

(12) long-term liability

(13) long-term loan

(14) debentures

(15) bond payable

(16) principal

(17) interest

(18) the maturity date

(19) accrued interest

(20) contingent liability

2. Please choose the word or phrase to fill the blanks.

(a) accounts payable	(d) unearned revenue	(g) management
(b) notes payable	(e) prepayment	(h) short-term
(c) a future event occurs	(f) shareholder	(i) long-term

(1) The account of________should be decreased when the service paid for in advance has been provided.

(2) The account of________should be recorded when the business purchased supplies on credit.

(3) The account of________used to show what the business owes the bank.

(4) Liabilities are what the business owes everyone except________.

(5) Contingent liabilities do not become liabilities unless________.

(6) Recording a utility bill payment for this accounting period will not increase________ liabilities.

3. Single choice question.

If a company issues a bond, the bond payable is listed on the balance sheet in the ( ).

A. non-current asset section

B. current liability section

C. non-current liability section

D. owners' equity section

4. Multiple choice question.

(1) Which of the following features belong to liability? (　　).

A. Result of past events

B. Present obligation

C. Potential obligation

D. The economic benefit will flow out of the business

(2) Which of the following accounting titles are current liabilities? (　　).

A. Account payable

B. Unearned revenue

C. Bond payable

D. Contingent liability

Chapter 6 Owner's Equity

Introduction

In Chapter 1, we have learned three types of business organization: sole trader, partnership and companies. A sole trader is a person who owns and runs the business. The income of the sole trader is distributed only to the owner. A partnership is an entity owned by two or more people. The income of the partnership is distributed according to the partnership agreement. Some partnerships distribute the income in proportion to the partners' investment, and some distribute the income equally to the partners. A company is an entity that has separate existence from that of its owners. Not like sole traders and partnerships, shareholders in a company are not personally liable for the debts of a corporation. So, the most that a stockholder may lose by investing in a corporation is the amount of his investment. For many investors, it is the most important advantage of a company comparing to sole traders and partnerships.

For the section of owner's equity in balance sheets are different in different countries. In some western countries, there are two items: capital stock and retained earnings. For more details, some balance sheets include detailed items of various preferred and common stock in capital stock section, and detailed items of dividends and other distributions in retained earnings section. In China, there are four sections in the owner's equity, i. e., paid-in capital, capital

stockholder 股票持有人
shareholder 股东
capital stock 股本
retained earnings 盈余；留存收益
dividends 股利；分红
paid-in capital 实收资本
capital surplus 资本公积
revenue surplus 收益盈余
undistributed profit 未分配利润

surplus, revenue surplus and undistributed profit.

Learning Objective

After studying this chapter, you should understand and be able to:

- ▶ Explain the definition of owners' equity.
- ▶ Make clear the difference between paid-in capital and retained earning.
- ▶ Explain the process of issuance of shares.
- ▶ Distinguish the difference between common stock and preferred stock.
- ▶ Explain the meaning of retained earnings.
- ▶ Distinguish the different types of dividends.

par value stock 有票面价值的股票

6.1 Definition of Owner's Equity

The amount by which business assets exceed business liabilities is called owner's equity. If there are no liabilities, the owner's equity is equal to the total amount of the assets. Owner's equity is increased with revenue, and decreased by expenses or an owner's withdrawal.

arbitrarily assigned 任意设定

Owner's equity in a company is defined as stockholders' equity, shareholders' equity, or corporate capital. The extract of owners' equity in balance sheet is shown below:

◎股东的长期投资就等于股东持有股数乘以每股票面价值。

Owners' equity	
Capital stock	600, 000
Capital surplus	80, 000
Retain earning	50, 000
Total stockholders' equity	730, 000

fair value 公允价值

Owners' equity normally includes the following three categories:

—Capital stock

—Additional paid-in capital (In China, it is called capital surplus.)

capital surplus 资本公积

—Retain earning (In China, it is called undistributed profit.)

Capital stock and additional paid-in capital constitute total "paid-in capital" while retained earnings represent the earned capital of the enterprise.

It is quite important to distinguish between paid-in capital and retained earnings in the balance sheet of a company. Only earnings of the company can be distributed as dividends by law. Companies cannot distribute dividends exceeding the cumulative balance in retained earnings so as to protect their creditors. We will first explain the accounts used to record paid-in capital transactions and then discuss retained earnings.

6.2 Paid-In Capital

Before we learn the detailed items in "paid-in capital" account, we need to know the different types of shares companies issued and how companies issue the share.

As we know, a corporation's capital is divided into shares with equal value and sold to the investors. The investors who hold the shares are called shareholders or stockholders. Many stocks have a par value. A firm may issue par value share or non-par value share.

6.2.1 Issuance of Shares

Par value stock

As we have learned in Chapter 5, par value of a bond stands for the amount that an issuer agrees to repay at the date of maturity. But the par value of a share is an arbitrarily assigned dollar amount. There is no relationship between the price at which a company issues stock, and the price at which the stocks trade in the marketplace, and the par value of the stock.

If the stock has "par value", stockholder's permanent investment is equal to the number of shares outstanding times the par value of each share.

no-par-value stock 无票面价值的股票

issued at a discount 折价发行

Sometimes a company may issue par value stock at a price in excess of par, then the stock is said to be issued at a premium.

Issuance of par value stock

When shares are issued, net assets and equity increase by fair value of assets given to the company. The capital stock account is credited for the par value of the stock issued. The excess value over par is credited to a descriptively named "paid-in capital in excess of par" account to record source in detail.

In China, we use the account called "capital surplus" instead of "paid-in capital in excess of par".

Illustration 6.1

The issuance of 100,000 shares of common stock, par \$1, for cash of \$1.2 per share. Please record this transaction.

Explanation: The par value of the share is \$1; the share was issued at premium for the price of \$1.5. So, the \$100,000 (100,000× \$1) should be credited to "capital stock" account, the \$50,000 (100,000×\$1.5−100,000×\$1) should be credited to "paid-in capital in excess of par" account or "capital surplus" account.

Answer:

Dr. Cash 150,000

  Cr. Capital Stock 100,000

    Paid-in Capital in Excess of Par (Capital Surplus) 50,000

No-par value stock

If the stock is "no-par value" stock, the shareholder's investment is an arbitrary amount that the board assigns to the stated capital account.

However, why does a company sometimes issue no-par value stock instead of par value stock? There are two main reasons. Firstly, a company may want to avoid the stocks being issued at a discount. Secondly, a company may want to avoid confusion over the relationship between the par value and fair market value.

Issuance of no-par value stock

When a company issues shares, no-par stock with a stated value is accounted for in the same manner as discussed for par value stock because the stated value places the no-par stock on essentially the same basis as par value stock.

No-par stock is recorded as a credit to the capital stock account. Therefore, the capital stock account should be credited for the full amount received. In this case, there is no "paid-in capital in excess" recorded. We can see, the accounting treatment of no-par value stock is different from par value stock.

Illustration 6.2

Assume that a company issues 20,000 shares of no-par common stock at $50 a share and at a later date issues 5,000 additional shares at $45. Please write down the accounting entries for these two transactions.

common shareholder 普通股股东

Explanation: The initial issuance value of no-par common stock is $50 per share; the number of share issued is 20,000. So the total value of these shares is $1,000,000 (20,000 × $50), which should be credited to "common stock" account. The later issuance value of no-par common stock is $45 per share; the number of share issued is 5,000. So the total value of these shares is $225,000 (5,000× $45), which should be credited to "common stock" account as well.

common stock 普通股

preferred stock 优先股

Answer:

Issued 20,000 shares of no-par common stock at $50:

Dr. Cash 1,000,000

  Cr. Common Stock 1,000,000

Issued 5,000 shares of no-par common stock at $45:

Dr. Cash 225,000

  Cr. Common Stock 225,000

6.2.2 The Rights of Common Shareholder and Preferred Shareholder

Rights of common shareholders

As we all know, shareholders are individual investors who purchase and own the shares of capital stock. They are the owners of a company. The ownership of a corporation can be divided into shares of capital stock. Capital stock is the number shares authorized for issuance by a company's charter, including both common stock and preferred stock. The interest of stockholders is determined by the number of shares that he or she owns.

Sometimes, companies issue more than one class of stock, such as common stock and preferred stock. The basic rights of these classes of shareholders are different. The following are the basic rights of common shareholders:

(1) Voting right

A stockholder has one vote for each share owned. They can vote for recruiting directors and on certain key issues. Shareholders are independent from managerial role unless they have been appointed by the board as a management role. The shareholder who owns more than 50% of the capital stock has the right to control the company. They can elect the board of directors and set basic corporate policies.

(2) Dividends & liquidation distribution right

A shareholder has the right to get dividends declared by the board of directors. The directors may elect to distribute some or all of the earnings of a profitable company to its shareholders in the form of cash dividends. Dividends can be distributed only after they have been formally declared by the board of directors and paid in proportion to the number of shares owned. Shareholders in a company could withdraw the company's assets when the corporation liquidates. After paying creditors, any remaining assets are divided among the shareholders again, in proportion to the number of shares owned.

(3) Preemptive right

A shareholder has the right to maintain his or her percentage ownership if the corporation increases the number of shares outstanding.

Rights of preferred shareholders

The rights of preferred shareholders are superior to those common

recruit 招聘
control the company 拥有公司的控制权
voting right 选举权
elect 选举
board of director 董事会
corporate polity 公司基本方针
dividends & liquidation distribution right 股利分配和清算参与权
preemptive right 优先购股权。若公司增发配股，股东有权利维持其所有权比例。
in arrears 之后

shareholders. These rights will pertain to either the earnings or the assets of the company. The preferred shares have the following features: ①participation in earnings beyond the stipulated dividend rate; ②a cumulative feature, affording the preferred shareholders the protection that their dividends in arrears, if any, will be fully satisfied before the common shareholders participate in any earnings distribution; ③convertibility or call ability by the corporation.

In exchange for the preferences, the preferred shareholders' rights are limited. The right to vote, and the right to participate without limitation in the earnings of the corporation, may be restricted to common shareholders.

6.3 Retained Earnings

The amount of retained earnings represents the cumulative net income of the firm since its beginning, less the total dividends that have been distributed to shareholders. The existence of retained earnings means that net assets generated by profitable operations have been kept in the company to help it grow or to meet other business needs. But a credit balance in retained earnings does not mean that cash or any designed set of assets is directly associated with retained earnings. The fact that earnings have been retained means that net assets as a whole have been increased.

Will the retained earnings carry a debit balance? The answer is yes. This may happen when a company losses and distributions to stockholders are greater than its profits from operations. In such a case, the firm is said to have a deficit (debit balance) in retained earnings. This is shown in the owner's equity section of the balance sheet as a deduction from paid-in capital.

6.3.1 Appropriated Retained Earnings

A company may voluntarily designate or bound by law or by con-

fair value 公允价值

outstanding share 发行在外的股票

voluntarily 自愿地

legal reserves 法定盈余

withdraw money 提取现金

cash dividend 现金分红

stock dividend 股票分红

board of directors 董事会

tract an amount of retained earnings for some special purpose as a means of explaining to stockholders why dividends are not being declared. In China companies must provide "legal reserves". Each year a certain percentage of income is appropriated if the corporation has net profit until the reserve amount equals 50% percentage of legal capital stockholders' equity. Thus, the main purpose of legal reserves is to protect creditors from overpayment of dividends and it is good for expansion. In the USA, appropriations of retained earnings are seldom seen on balance sheets. Instead, management's reasons for not declaring dividends usually are conveyed in a letter to stockholders that is published with the financial statements.

6. 3. 2 Dividends

If you had your own small business and wanted to withdraw money for personal use, you would simply withdraw it from the company's account. In a company, a formal action by the board of directors is required before money can be distributed to the owners. The distributions to owners or investors are called dividends. Dividends usually have two forms: cash dividends and stock dividends.

6. 3. 2. 1 Cash Dividends

A cash distribution of earnings by a company to its shareholders is called a cash dividend, which is the most common form of dividend distribution. A company that has large amount of retained earnings does not always mean this company has enough cash available for paying dividends. On the other hand, a company's board of directors is not required by law to declare dividends. Company's earnings may have been invested in new plant and equipment, or in paying off debts, etc. This could happen even if both retained earnings and cash are large enough to justify a dividend.

However, if a company wants to attract their investors, they will try to maintain the dividend distributed on a stable level. How much dividend can a company distribute to its shareholders? It depends on the retained earnings limit, which is the total undistributed net in-

a stable level 一个稳定水平

announce dividend declarations 宣告分发股利

dilute 稀释

come. A company can announce dividend declarations in financial newspapers or when providing investors service.

6. 3. 2. 2 Stock Dividends

A stock distribution of earnings by a corporation to its shareholders is called stock distribution. Comparing to cash distribution, stock distributions do not distribute cash or other assets to shareholders. Such distributions are in common stock form and are issued to common shareholders. This will increase every shareholder's number of shares by the same percentage. For the tax issue, cash dividends are taxable, while stock dividends are often not taxable until the shares are sold.

The influence of a stock dividend distribution on owner's equity is to transfer the retained earnings to paid-in capital account. The value of transferring from retained earnings to paid-in capital account is normally the fair value of the shares. Thus, we can see, distribution of stock dividend does not change the balance of income, assets, or owners' equity, but it increases the number of outstanding shares. Subsequently, it will dilute the company's share. In other words, the market price per share will decrease.

The double entries to record a stock dividend in USA and China are quite different. In China, the accounting record of all stock dividends are the same no matter large or small stock dividends. The accounting entry of stock dividends is recorded at the date of payment. And the stock dividends should disclose in the financial statement.

In USA, the accounting entries to record a stock dividend depend on the issuance size. If a company declares stock more than 25%, it is called large stock dividend. This will increase the number of shares available in the market and usually lower the stock price. If a company declares stock less than 25%, it is called small stock divided. Therefore, to record a stock dividend, the debit side is recorded in the "retained earnings" account with the fair value of the additional shares issued, and the credit side is recorded in the "paid-in capital in excess of par" account.

balance 余额
declare 宣告
stock dividend 股票股利

Illustration 6.3

ABC Company has a balance of $50,000 in retained earnings and 60,000 shares of $10 par value common stock. The current fair value of its stock is $12 per share.

1) If ABC Company declares a 10% stock dividend, what is the accounting entries of this transaction?

2) If ABC Company declares a 40% stock dividend, what is the accounting entries of this transaction?

***Explanation*:**

The accounting entries in USA and China are different. In USA, when ABC Company declares 10% stock dividend, it is small stock dividend. The credit side should include the common stock capital in par value and the paid-in capital in excess of par. The debit side should be retained earning including the above two values. However, when ABC Company declares 40% stock dividend, it is large stock dividend. The credit side only includes the common stock capital in par value. The debit side should be retained earning including only common stock value at par value.

In China, the accounting entries of all stock dividends are the same as large stock dividends treatment in USA. Thus, the credit side only includes common stock capital in par value. The debit side should be retained earning including only common stock value at par value.

***Answer*:**

In USA:

1) Declares a 10% stock dividend:

The date of declaration		
Dr. Retained Earnings	72,000	
Cr. Common Stock to Be Distributed		60,000
Paid-In Capital in Excess of Par		12,000
The date of payment		
Dr. Common Stock to Be Distributed	60,000	
Cr. Common Stock		60,000

2) Declares a 40% stock dividend:

The declaration date	
Dr. Retained Earnings	240, 000
Cr. Common Stock to Be Distributed	240, 000
The date of payment	
Dr. Common Stock to Be Distributed	240, 000
Cr. Common Stock	240, 000

payment of dividend 股利发放

dividend payable 应付股利

In China:

1) Declares a 10% stock dividend

The date of declaration:

Dr. Retained Earnings 60, 000

Cr. Common Stock to Be Distributed 60, 000

The date of payment:

Dr. Common Stock to Be Distributed 60, 000

Cr. Common Stock 60, 000

2) Declares a 40% stock dividend

The declaration date:

Dr. Retained Earnings 240, 000

Cr. Common Stock to Be Distributed 240, 000

The date of payment:

Dr. Common Stock to Be Distributed 240, 000

Cr. Common Stock 240, 000

6.3.2.3 Dividend Declaration

A company will not pay dividend automatically and the board of directors needs to declare a dividend. From declaration to payment of dividend, there are three important dates related to dividends: the declaration date, the record date and the payment date. Normally, there is a time span of two to four weeks between dates. The accounting entries are required on those three dates.

On the declaration date, the board of directors announces the intention to pay the dividend. The declaration creates a liability for the corporation and the temporary account "dividend" introduces.

So, the dividend account should be debited and the dividend payable should be credited when a company declares. At the end of the accounting year, the record date, the balance in the dividends account is closed by transferring the account balance to retained earnings. On payment date, payment of dividend is recorded by debiting dividends payable, and crediting cash.

Illustration 6.4

On December 1, 2019, the directors of ABC Company declared a 50 cents per share cash dividend on 100,000 shares of $10 par value common stock.

The company paid the dividend on January 31, 2020. What are the accounting entries for this transition?

stock split 股票分割

proportionate number 一定比例数量

Explanation:

We should make three entries on the date of declaration, the date of record and the date of payment.

Answer:

On the date of declaration	
Dr. Dividends	50,000
Cr. Dividends payable	50,000
On the end of the year	
Dr. Retained earnings	50,000
Cr. Dividends	50,000
On the payment date	
Dr. Dividends payable	50,000
Cr. Cash	50,000

We can see from the illustration, the cumulative effect of the declaration and payment of a cash dividend on a company's financial statement is to decrease both stockholders' equity and total assets.

6.3.2.4 Stock Split

Companies sometimes reduce the par or stated value of their common stock and issue a proportionate number of additional shares. This process is said to split its stock, and it is called a stock split. A stock split is an increase in the number of outstanding shares of a company's stock, so that proportionate equity of each shareholder remains the same. That means a stock split does not change the total par or stated value of the stock. Therefore, there is no transfer made from retained earnings to common stock when a stock split is affected.

The following table makes a comparison of stock dividends and stock split:

Stock Dividends	Stock Split
Par value of a share does not change	Par value of a share decreases
Total number of shares increases	Total number of shares increases
Total owners' equity does not change	Total owners' equity does not change
The composition of equity changes	The composition of equity does not change
Stock dividends require journal entries	Stock split do not require journal entries

Exercise 6

1. Please translate the following terms into Chinese.

(1) distribution

(2) divide

(3) share

(4) issuance

(5) common stock

(6) preferred stock

(7) shareholder (stockholder)

(8) dividend

(9) preemptive right

(10) par value stock

(11) no-par value stock

(12) paid-in capital

(13) additional paid-in capital

(14) capital surplus

(15) retained earnings

(16) cash dividend

(17) stock dividend

(18) declaration of dividend

(19) dividend distribution

(20) stock split

2. Please choose the word or phrase to fill the blanks.

(a) cash dividend	(d) owners' equity	(g) par value
(b) common stock	(e) stock dividend	(h) stock split
(c) market value	(f) retained earnings	(i) preferred

(1) A company's balance sheet includes assets, liabilities, and________.

(2) ________and________are the two common capital stocks issued by a company.

(3) ________and________are the usual forms of distribution to shareholders.

(4) ________is the legal value of a share of stock.

(5) ________represents the company's accumulated net income, less accumulated dividends and other amounts transferred to paid-in capital accounts.

(6) ________is an increase in the number of outstanding shares of a company's stock.

3. Single choice question.

(1) Cash dividends are paid on the basis of the number of shares ( ).

A. authorized

B. issued

C. outstanding

D. outstanding less the number of treasury shares

(2) If a company repurchases its own share, the share is listed on the balance sheet in the ( ).

A. current assets section

B. long-term liability section

C. owners' equity section

D. current liability section

4. Multiple choice question.

(1) Which of the following is a characteristic of equity rather than liabilities? ( ).

A. The obligation matures

B. Interest paid to the provider of the capital is deductible in the determination of taxable income

C. The capital providers' claims are residual in the event of liquidation of the business

D. The capital providers normally have the right to exercise control over business operations

(2) Paid-in capital for a corporation may arise from which of the following sources? ( ).

A. Issuing cumulative preferred stock

B. Receiving donations of real estate

C. Selling the corporation's treasury stock

D. Distribution of dividend

(3) The owners' equity section of the balance sheet may include ( ).

A. common stock

B. paid-in capital

C. retained earnings

D. revenue

5. Make the correct items by "T" and the wrong items by "F".

(1) Par value is strictly a legal matter, and it establishes the legal capital of a corporation. ( )

(2) A stock is issued at a premium when the par exceeds the selling price. ( )

(3) A company must, by law, pay a dividend once a year. ( )

(4) Dividends are an expense of a corporation and should be charged to the periodic income. ( )

(5) Appropriation of retained earnings has no effect on total owners' equity. ( )

Chapter 7 Revenue and Expense

Introduction

When mentioning the revenue, most of us will think of sales revenue. However, there are three types of revenues: sales revenue, service revenue and other operating revenue. Sales revenue occur when you sell products to customers. The sales revenue can be recognized when the economic benefits associated with the transaction flow to the enterprise and the relevant amount of revenue and cost can be measured reliably. The amount of sales revenue is determined by the value stipulated in the contract or agreement signed by the enterprise and the buyer or agreed amount. The service revenue occurs when you provide service to customers. Usually, the service is determined by the stage of completion of the service. The sales revenue and service revenue are prime operating revenues of an enterprise. Besides, revenue can rise from lease of asset and remised right of asset, etc.

sales revenue 销售收入

service revenue（提供）服务的收入

operating revenue 经营性收入

be measured reliably 可以可靠地计量

The expense is usually divided into product expenses and period expenses. Product expenses are direct cost while period expenses are indirect cost including operating expense, administrative expense and finance expense.

Learning Objectives

After studying this chapter, you should understand or be able to:

▶ Explain the definition of revenue;

▶ Recognition of revenue;

- Explain the definition of expense;
- Know the types of expenses.

7.1 Revenue

Revenue is the gross inflow of economic benefit arising during the ordinary activities of an enterprise from such events as the sale of goods, the rendering of service and the use of enterprises by others. Revenue growth is an important indicator of the market reception of a company's products and services.

sales of goods 销售货物
rendering of service 提供服务

Revenue is also referred to as sales or income. It forms the beginning of a corporation's income statement and is often considered the "Top Line" of a business.

Types of Revenue

Revenues increase owners' equity. The inflow of receivable and cash from customers increases the total assets of the company; on the other side of the accounting equation, the liabilities do not change, but owners' equity is increased to match the increase in total assets. Thus revenue is the gross increase in owners' equity resulting from business transaction.

susceptible 可疑的
manipulation 操作
bias 偏差

The revenue can be divided into sales revenue, service revenue and other operation revenue.

IFRS 国际财务报告准则

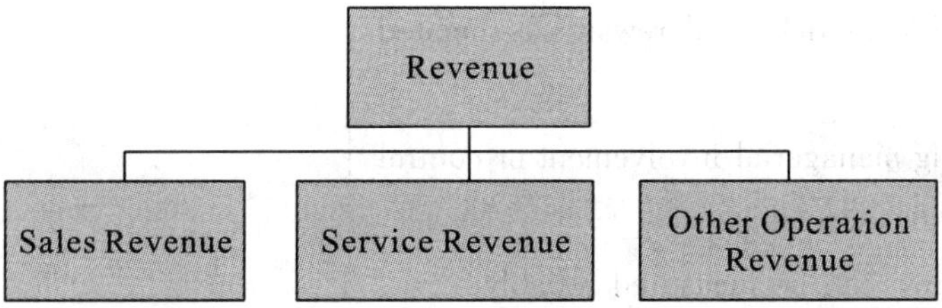

Sales Revenue

Sales revenue arises from the sale of goods. When an accountant confirms sales revenue, several conditions must be noticed. Firstly, the enterprise has transferred the significant risks to the buyer. Secondly, the enterprise cannot retain continuing managerial involvement to the degree usually associated with ownership.

Service Revenue

Sales revenue arises from providing of services. When services provided are started and completed within the same accounting year, revenue should be recognized at the time of completion of the services. To calculate the revenue, the conditions of transactions and computing methods are very important. An accountant needs to make sure that the total amount of service revenue and costs of completion of the services provided can be measured reliably. Besides, the economic benefit will flow to the enterprise.

Other Operating Revenue

Other operating revenues usually arise from wrappage lease, remising right of assets, using of enterprise assets by others, etc. In order to recognize other operating revenues, the economic benefits associated with the transaction will flow to the enterprise, and the amount of the revenue can be measured reliably.

Revenue Recognition for the Sale of Goods

The revenue recognition is the process and timing by which revenue is recorded and recognized as an item in a company's financial statements. In accounting, revenue recognition is one of the areas that is most susceptible to manipulation and bias.

According to IFRS, all of the following five conditions must be met for a company to recognize revenue:

· There is a transfer of significant risks and rewards associated with ownership.

· There is a loss of continuing managerial involvement or control to the degree usually associated with ownership.

· The amount of revenue inflow can be measured reliably.

economic benefit 经济利益

delivery 发货

on credit 提供信用

sale on credit 赊销

construction contract 建造合同

· It is probable that economic benefits will flow to the seller.

· The costs incurred or the costs to be incurred can be measured reliably.

Cash Sale

For the sale of goods, most of the time, revenue is recognized upon delivery. This is because, at the time of delivery, all five criteria are met. The accounting entry should be:

Dr. Cash/Bank/Accounts Receivable/Note Receivable ××

  Cr. Revenue ××

When revenue is recognized, according to the matching principle, expenses must also be considered for:

Dr. Cost of Goods Sold ××

  Cr. Inventory ××

Let's take an example:

In August, ABC Company sold $500,000 worth of goods to customers on credit. The Cost of Goods Sold (COGS) is 80%. What should the accounting entries for this transaction be?

Answer:

Revenue recognized:

Dr. Accounts Receivable 500,000

  Cr. Revenue 500,000

Corresponding costs:

Dr. Cost of Goods Sold 400,000

  Cr. Inventory 400,000

Installment Sale

Installment sales are quite common, where products are sold on a deferred payment plan and payments are received in the future after the goods have already been delivered to the customer. Property such as appliances, equipment, materials, real estate, and many other types of merchandise may be sold on an installment basis. The installment sales refer to a plan whereby the seller agrees to give the buyer physical possession of the goods in exchange for a promise to make payments periodically over a specified time interval. The agreement

cost of goods sold (COGS) 销售成本

fixed price contract 固定价格合同

cost-plus contracts 成本加成合同

between the buyer and the seller is reflected in legal terms as a conditional sales contract. Usually, the price of installment sale is higher than cash sale, because it offsets the added risk imposed on the seller for waiting to collect payments and the additional record-keeping expenses involved. Under this method, revenue can only be recognized when the actual cash is collected from the customer.

We shall see another example:

In August, Bee Company sold $500,000 worth of goods to customers on credit. In September, $100,000 was collected and in October, another $100,000 was collected. The COGS is 80%. What should the accounting entries during the installment sale be?

Answer:

In August, when selling the goods

Dr. Instalment Accounts Receivable	500,000
Cr. Deferred Revenue	500,000
Dr. Deferred COGS	400,000
Cr. Inventory	400,000

In September, the first $100,000 was collected

Dr. Cash 100,000
  Cr. Installment Accounts Receivable 100,000
Dr. Deferred Revenue 100,000
  Cr. Sales Revenue 100,000
Dr. COGS 80,000
  Cr. Deferred COGS 80,000

In October, another $100,000 was collected

Dr. Deferred Revenue 100,000
  Cr. Sales Revenue 100,000
Dr. COGS 80,000
  Cr. Deferred COGS 80,000

Revenue Recognition for Provision of Services

When mentioning the provision of services, one important area is the construction contracts. These are contracts to construct an asset

revenue recognition 确认收入

fixed price contract 固定价格的合同

or a combination of assets such as large ships, office buildings, and other projects that usually span multiple years.

In recognizing revenue for service provided over a long period of time, according to IFRS, revenue should be recognized based on the progress towards completion, also referred to as the percentage of completion method.

These contracts are of two kinds: fixed price contracts and cost-plus contracts. In fixed price contracts, the contractor agrees to a price before construction actually begins. Thus, all the risks are imposed on the contractor. In cost-plus contracts, the price depends on the amount actually spent on the project plus a profit margin. Dissimilar to the percentage of completion method, the completed contract method only allows revenue recognition when the contract is completed.

7.2　Expenses

Expenses refer to the outlays incurred by an enterprise during the course of production and operation. It means the outflows or other using up of assets or incurrence of liabilities during a period. An expense is a type of expenditure that flows through the income statement and is deducted from revenue to arrive at net income. Due to accrual principle in accounting, expenses are recognized when they are incurred, not necessarily when they are paid for. According to different standard, expenses can be divided into operating expense and non-operating expense, fixed expense and variable expense, revenue expense and capital expense.

Operating Expense VS. Non-operating Expense

The main different between operating expenses and non-operating expenses is that operating expenses are the expenses incur in the daily operating business while non-operating expenses are not. The main example of those two expenses are as follows.

cost plus contract 成本加成合同
outflows 流出
using up of asset 资产的消耗
incurrence of liability 产生负债
expenditure 支出
deduct 扣减
operating expense 经营费用
non-operating expense 非经营费用
fixed expense 固定费用

1） Operating Expense

· Cost of goods sold （COGS）

· Marketing， advertising， and promotion

· Salaries， benefits， and wages

· Selling， general， and administrative

· Rent and insurance

· Depreciation and amortization

· Other

2） Non-operating Expense

· Interest

· Taxes

· Impairment charges

Fixed Expense VS. Variable Expense

Fixed expenses are expenditure incurred in a fixed time. However， variable expense means the expenditure incurred occasionally. The examples of those two expenses are as follows.

1） Fixed Expense

· Rent

· Salaries， benefit， and wages （sometimes fixed and sometimes variable）

2） Variable Expense

· Transaction fees

· Commissions

· Marketing and advertising （sometimes fixed and sometimes variable）

Revenue Expense and Capital Expense

The only difference between revenue expense and capital expense is that a revenue expense has been recognized under the accrual principle and is reflected on the income statement， whereas a capital expense goes straight to balance sheet as an asset.

Once a capital expenditure goes on the balance sheet as an asset， it can be expensed later as depreciation and amortization， which flows through the income statement.

variable expense 变动费用
impairment 减值
transaction fee 交易手续费
commission 佣金
revenue expense （与收入相关的）费用
capital expense 资本性支出（资产）
product expenses（与生产产品相关的）费用
direct material cost 直接材料成本
direct labour cost 直接人工成本
indirect cost 间接成本
manufacturing process 生产过程
manufacturing overhead 生产的间接费用（制造费用）
water and electricity expenses 水电费
leasing charges 租金
maintenance 维修费

Product Expense, Indirect Expense and Period Expense

Product expenses are directly related to the products, which are composed of direct material costs, direct labour costs and indirect costs. Direct material costs are raw material costs. Direct labour costs mean the wages and salaries of the personal connected with manufacturing process.

Indirect expenses mainly refer to manufacturing overhead, such as water and electricity expenses, leasing charges, maintenance and so on.

Period expenses are not directly associated with products, but they are indispensable for generating the current revenue. Period expenses are composed of operating expense, administrative expense and so on.

Now, let's take the example of ABC CO. for illustration.

Below is an example of ABC CO.'s 2017 income statement (statement of operation) which lists their main categories of expense. As you can see, ABC CO. separates its costs into two categories.

Operating expenses consist of cost of sales, fulfilment, marketing, technology and content, general and administrative, and other.

Non-operating expenses comprise interest expense (and income), and other expense (income). Finally, ABC CO. has charged a provision for income taxes and accounted for equity method investment activity.

period expense 期间费用

separate 分成

category 种类

cost of sales 销售成本

fulfilment 完成

marketing expense 市场开发费用

technology and content expenses 技术和内容开支

general and administrative expense 管理费用

interest expense 利息费用

equity method 权益法

ABC CO, INC.
CONSOLIDATED STATEMENTS OF OPERATIONS
(In $ millions, except per share data)

	Year Ended December 31	
	2017	2018
Net product sales	79,268	94,665
Net service sales	27,738	41,322
Total net sales	107,006	135,987
Operating expenses:		
Cost of sales	71,651	88,265
Fulfillment	13,410	17,619
Marketing	5,254	7,233
Technology and content	12,540	16,085
General and administrative	1,747	2,432
Other operating expenses, net	171	167
Total Operating expenses	104,773	131,801
Operating income	2,233	4,186
Interest income	50	100
Interest expense	-459	-484
Other income (expense), net	-256	90
Total non-operating income (expense)	-665	-294
Income before income taxes	1,568	3,892
Provision for income taxes	-950	-1,425
Equity-method investment activity, net of tax	-22	-96
Net income	596	2,371

Exercise 7

1. Phrase translation.

(1) sales revenue

(2) service revenue

(3) prime operating revenue

(4) provide service

(5) product expense

(6) direct material cost

(7) direct labor cost

(8) manufacturing overhead

(9) leasing charge

(10) maintenance

(11) period expense

(12) administration expense

(13) finance expense

(14) freight charges

(15) advertising expenses

2. Phrase matching.

(a) sales revenue	(d) service revenue	(g) sales expensess
(b) other operation revenue	(e) finance expenses	(h) revenue
(c) administrative expense	(f) product costs	(i) expense

(1) ________arises from the sale of goods.

(2) ________arises from rendering services.

(3) Period expenses include________, ________and________.

(4) ________are directly related to the products, which are composed of direct material costs, direct labour costs and the indirect costs.

(5) ________causes an increase in owner's equity.

(6) ________causes an decrease in owner's equity.

3. Single choice.

(1) Production costs include direct material cost, direct labor costs and (　　).

A. insurance cost

B. promotion cost

C. administration cost

D. manufacturing overhead

(2) Period costs are composed of sales expense, administrative expense and ( ).

A. labor cost

B. material cost

C. finance cost

D. production overhead

4. Multiple choice.

(1) Which of the following can be recognized as revenue? ( ).

A. Sales revenue

B. Interest income

C. Rent income

D. Freight charges

(2) Revenue can be recognised when ( ).

A. the economic associated with the transaction flows to the enterprise

B. all the economic benefits flow to the enterprise

C. the revenue can be measured reliably

D. the relevant amount of revenue and costs can be measured reliably

5. True or false.

(1) Revenue increases owner's equity. ( )

(2) Revenue is recognized when we receive cash from the buyers. ( )

(3) Advertising expense is usually collected as period expense. ( )

(4) Sales returns should be recorded as a reduction of revenue. ( )

(5) If revenues exceed expenses for the same accounting period, the entity is deemed to suffer a loss. ( )

Chapter 8 The Impact of Typical Transactions on the Financial Statements

Introduction

In the previous chapters, we have introduced the different types of organizations, the fundamental framework, the financial statements and the basic elements of the financial statements. We also managed to understand the process of recording financial information in the accounts, journalizing and posting, and generating financial statements. Now, in this chapter, we shall take further look at the financial statements, to get better understanding of the impact of transactions on the financial statements and how we can analyze the financial statements with known information.

When a company is established, all the transactions occurred would give result to the change of the financial statements, such as starting a business, borrowing from the bank, purchasing tangible assets, intangible assets and inventories, and selling products. In this part, let's find out how these typical transactions may impact our financial statements.

analyze the financial statement 分析财务报表
known information 已知信息
start a business 创办公司
borrow money from the bank 从银行取得贷款
purchase tangible assets 购买有形资产
selling products 销售产品

8.1 Establishing a Company

The shareholders invest 20 million dollars to start a company. Remark, the shareholders give 20 million dollars in the form of real money. What does it mean?

It means, the money, that can be utilized to do the business, is now in place. Think about it: Does this event increase the amount of cash and cash equivalent? The answer is Yes!

In the financial statement, we cannot merely record the change in only one account. As we know, every transaction that occurs will impact at least two accounts, and that can be also explained by the double-entry rule. So, when we recognize the increase in the cash and cash equivalent, and asset items, we should answer the other question: Where does the money come from? Well, the money is invested by the shareholder, and according to the accounting equivalent:

Assets = Liabilities + Equity

The investment will not be repaid by capital plus interests, and it does not count as a borrowing, so it will not be recognized as a liability. Clearly, an equity will be recognized in the balance sheet. In this event, it increases both the asset and the equity in the balance sheet. And that's how the transaction impact our first financial statement. The double entry would be:

Dr. Bank 20, 000, 000

Cr. Capital 20, 000, 000

Does this transaction impact the income statement? The answer is "no". The income statement complies with the rule: Revenue−Expense = Profit. Obviously, the investment event is not a sales activity, thus it will not impact the income statement. It should be remarked that, there are two kinds of assets that can realize profit or loss without being involved in the selling process. The first kind is the exchange rate changes in cash and cash equivalent giving rise to profit or loss. The other kind is the financial assets measured at fair value through profit and loss, which means the changes in fair value will be recognized in profit or loss. Both items are not about the sales, but will cause the changes in the income statement either way.

So, the above is about the impact of the first kind of transaction on the financial statements.

◎股东投资企业，一方面带来货币资金的增加，另一方面带来权益的增加。按照会计恒等式“资产=负债+权益”，该项业务不会影响到利润表项目的变化。

sales activity 销售业务

fair value 公允价值

STATEMENT OF FINANCIAL POSITION ON 31 DEC. 2015

unit: $ million

Assets		
Cash		20
Total Assets		20
Liabilities		
Total Liabilities		
Owners' Equity		
Capital Stock		20
Total Liabilities and Owners' Equity		20

8.2 Borrowing from Bank

The company borrows 10 million dollars for 6 months from bank. Based on the previous event, we can better understand this transaction. The borrowing as well gives rise to the increase in cash and cash equivalent. We also think about the question: Where does the money come from? As we know, the money borrowed from bank shall be repaid with capital and interests as it is due, hence the money borrowed should be considered as a liability in the balance sheet.

And we see that, when a company is started and requires funds to do business, they can finance the funds through both liability and equity.

◎企业除了可以发行股票进行股权融资以外，还可以向商业银行申请贷款，进行债务融资。同样地，货币资金会增加，因为钱“到手了”，但不同的是，货币资金对应的不再是权益类科目，而是负债类科目，这是对于股权融资和债务融资我们应该区分的地方。该项业务仍然不会影响利润表。

STATEMENT OF FINANCIAL POSITION AT 31 DEC. 2015

unit: $ million

Assets		
Cash		20+10
Total Assets		20+10
Liabilities		
Bank Loan		10
Total Liabilities		10
Owners' Equity		
Capital Stock		20
Total Liabilities and Owners' Equity		20+10

8.3 Purchasing Intangible Assets

Due to the previous events, the company has the money to start its business. Now, the company is purchasing a manufacturing license for 2 million dollars. The event causes an increase in intangible assets and a decrease in cash and cash equivalent, and there will be no changes in the income statement. Here, we do not need to think about whether the money we spend is from the shareholder or the bank. This transaction reflects the form change of the assets. The decrease in one asset gives rise to the increase in another asset. Namely, 2 million dollars has been spent to acquire the license.

It should be noticed that, even such transaction will not cause any change in the income statement at its initial measurement. However, subsequent measurement will do as amortized cost will be expensed during the period of benefit.

STATEMENT OF FINANCIAL POSITION ON 31 DEC. 2015

unit: $ million

Assets		
Cash		20+10−2
Patents		2
Total Assets		20+10−2
Liabilities		
Bank Loan		10
Total Liabilities		10
Owners' Equity		
Capital Stock		20
Total Liabilities and Owners' Equity		20+10

◎企业融资后，有了流动资金，可以购买无形资产，如商标、产权等。这项业务涉及无形资产的增加和货币资金的减少。同为资产类项目，一增一减，资产负债表依然平衡。注意：该项业务在采购时不会影响利润表，只会带来资产类项目内部的变化。但是后期无形资产会根据受益年限进行摊销，计入损益表。

◎企业融资后，有了流动资金，还可以购买有形资产，如房产、汽车等。同上一项业务，一项资产增加带来另一项资产减少。

◎这项业务在采购时不会引起利润表变化，但是后期会根据受益年限进行折旧，折旧费计入利润表。

generate future cash inflow 产生未来现金流

8.4 Purchasing Tangible Assets

Tangible assets such as equipment and plant, are non-current assets with substance, owned by the company, to generate future cash inflow. The company is now purchasing properties and equipments for 6 million. Similar to the last event of purchasing intangible assets, this even would also cause the increase in one asset item and the decrease in another. Hence, the tangible assets will rise while the amount of cash goes down. And there will be no change to the statement of profit or loss.

Similar to the intangible assets acquirement case, the subsequent measurement of tangible assets will give rise to changes in the income statement, as a result of depreciation cost incurred over time.

◎企业使用自有资金采购存货，货币资金减少的同时，存货增加。报表平衡。

◎注意：在采购存货时，并不确认成本，所以不会影响利润表。

STATEMENT OF FINANCIAL POSITION ON 31 DEC. 2015

unit: $ million

Assets		
Cash		20+10-2-6
Patents		2
Property, Plant & Equipment		6
Total Assets		20+10
Liabilities		
Bank Loan		10
Total Liabilities		10
Owners' Equity		
Capital Stock		20
Total Liabilities and Owners' Equity		20+10

8.5 Purchasing Inventories

With the necessary license and properties and plants to manufacture products, the company can now be able to buy the inventories to start the next process. The company purchased 2 million inventories for future selling. Remember that, when we are dealing with anything that is in relation with money, always think about that: where does the money go? In this situation, the money goes to the supplier, thus the inventory is in stock. For now the inventory is purchased but not sold yet, so that it will not influence the income statement. Its impact on the statement of financial position will be presented as:

STATEMENT OF FINANCIAL POSITION ON 31 DEC. 2015

unit: $ million

Assets		
Cash		20+10-2-6-2
Patent		2
Property, Plant & Equipment		6
Inventory		2
Total Assets		20+10
Liabilities		
Bank Loan		10
Total Liabilities		10
Owners' Equity		
Capital Stock		20
Total Liabilities and Owners' Equity		20+10

◎企业销售产品，一方面确认收入、应收款项或货币资金，另一方面结转产品的成本，确认减少的存货和增加的成本。收入和成本的差异就是利润的体现。

book value 账面价值

recognize 确认

8.6 Selling Products

The company sold part of the inventory at 1.5 million dollars in credit for 3 months, with its book value of 1 million dollars. It is easy to analyze this transaction. On one hand, the products are sold even though the payment has not been paid, and the revenue should be recognized according to accrual basis. On the other hand, as the inventories are sold, the cost should be carried over. The difference between the selling price and the cost of goods sold is the profit that should be recognized.

When the revenue is recognized, sales will be recorded in the income statement. As we know, the products are sold in credit and the payment has not yet been made, then what should be recorded on the other side of the double entry? The money is not received yet, hence we cannot record it in cash account. The transaction gives the company a right to receive the money in 3 months so that it can be considered as creditor's right and recorded as account receivable.

sold in credit 赊销（已销售但未收到款）

a right to receive the money in 3 months 在未来 3 个月内有权收取款项

After the revenue is recognized, the cost should be recognized as well. The corresponding inventory account will be carried over to the cost of goods sold account.

corresponding 相应的

So the sales transaction will influence both the balance sheet and the income statement.

STATEMENT OF FINANCIAL POSITION ON 31 DEC. 2015

unit: $ million

Assets		
Cash		20+10−2−6−2
Patent		2
Property, Plant & Equipment		6
Inventory		2−1
Account Receivable		1.5
Total Assets		20+10−1+1.5−1
Liabilities		
Bank Loan		10
Total Liabilities		10
Owners'Equity		
Capital Stock		20
Retained Earnings		0.5
Total Liabilities and Owners' Equity		20+10

STATEMENT OF PROFIT AND LOSS FOR THE YEAR ENDED 31 DEC. 2015

unit: $ million

Sales	1.5
Less: Cost of Goods Sold	1
Gross Profits on Sales	0.5

Exercise 8

1. Single choices.

(1) Which is not the means of financing in a newly starting business? (　　).

A. Borrowing money from banks and other financial institutions

B. Issuing capital stock from shareholders

C. Shareholders invest with an agreed amount of money

D. Government's subsidy to the business

(2) Which is not an element of the statement of financial position? (　　).

A. Liabilities

B. Equity

C. Asset

D. Profit

(3) Purchasing an intangible asset with cash will impact (　　).

A. The statement of profit or loss

B. The intangible asset account balance in the statement of financial position

C. The total asset of the business

D. The total equity of the business

2. Translate the following items into Chinese.

(1) start a business

(2) borrow money from the bank

(3) purchase intangible asset

(4) cost of goods sold

(5) sold in credit

(6) generate future cash inflow

(7) book value

(8) fair value

(9) statement of profit or loss

(10) selling activity

Chapter 9 Interpretation of Financial Statements

The financial statements of a company record important financial data on every aspect of a business's activities. As such they can be evaluated on the basis of past, current, and projected performance.

In general, financial statements are centered around generally accepted accounting principles (GAAP) in the U.S. These principles require a company to create and maintain three main financial statements: the balance sheet, the income statement, and the cash flow statement. Public companies have stricter standards for financial statement reporting. Public companies must follow GAAP standards which require accrual accounting. Private companies have greater flexibility in their financial statement preparation and they also have the option to use either accrual or cash accounting.

The basic financial statements provide much of the information for the users who need to make economic decisions about the businesses. In this chapter, we aim to explain the basic source of financial statement analysis, learn how to calculate accounting ratios and know how these ratios are used to analyze financial statements. Then we can develop the ability to analyze the financial statements of an organization, and describe the importance of financial analysis when making decisions.

generally accepted accounting principles (GAAP) 通用会计准则

◎财务报表的使用者范围很广，包括公司的管理层、投资人、债权人以及其他利益相关者。

◎投资人是公司股权的持有者，他们通过持有股票并根据股票价值的变化实现自身利益。

9.1 Objectives of Financial Statements Interpretation

The main analysts of financial statements mainly fall into two board categories: the internal analysts and the external analysts. The management level of an entity is the main internal analysts while the external analysts include investors, creditors and other stakeholders. In this chapter, we mainly focus on the external analysts.

The investors are actual or potential purchasers of capital stock of the company. They tend to receive dividends and realize an increase in their wealth by an increase in the value of stock or an increase in the net assets of the invested company. Hence, they expect to use financial statement analysis to make decisions related to their objectives.

The creditors who make loans to the company, also, expect to receive interests and principal during times. They need to know the safety of principals and the interests according to financial statements analysis.

All these stakeholders may analyze the financial statements in three ways:

Evaluate the past performance;

Assess the current financial position;

Judge the future developing potentialities and related risks.

9.2 Basic Analytical Procedures

With the information prepared in the financial statements, analytical procedures are carried by the analysts in order to test the current position, assets management, solvency ability and profitability of the entity. Horizontal analysis, vertical analysis and

calculate 计算

analyze the financial statements 分析财务报表

internal analyst 内部分析师

external analyst 外部分析师

◎债权人向公司提供借款，通过合同现金流收取本金和利息。

◎报表使用者将关注企业过去的、当前的财务和经营状况，评价并预测未来的机遇和风险。

vertical analysis 垂直分析法。垂直分析法用百分比表述报表的每一个组成部分与整体之间的关系。可以在表中反映各个项目变化的详细情况，百分比分析可以基于合计数进行。

ratio analysis are basis analytical procedures that are usually taken by analysts and will be introduced.

9.2.1 Vertical Analysis

Vertical analysis is a method of financial statement analysis in which each line item is listed as a percentage of a base figure within the statement. Thus, line items on an income statement can be stated as a percentage of gross sales, while line items on a balance sheet can be stated as a percentage of total assets or liabilities, and vertical analysis of a cash flow statement shows each cash inflow or outflow as a percentage of the total cash inflows.

Vertical analysis makes it much easier to compare the financial statements of one company with another, and across industries. This is because one can see the relative proportions of account balances. It is also easier to compare previous periods for time series analysis, in which quarterly and annual figures are compared over a number of years, in order to gain a hologram of whether performance metrics are improving or deteriorating.

For example, by showing the various expense line items in the income statement as a percentage of sales, one can see how these are contributing to profit margins and whether profitability is improving over time. It thus becomes easier to compare the profitability of a company with its peers.

Financial statements that include vertical analysis clearly show line item percentages in a separate column. These types of financial statements, including detailed vertical analysis, are also known as common-size financial statements and are used by many companies to provide greater detail on a company's financial position. Common-size financial statements often incorporate comparative financial statements that include columns comparing each line item to a previously reported period.

9.2.2 Horizontal Analysis

Horizontal analysis is used in financial statement analysis to com-

horizontal analysis 水平分析法。水平分析法多利用百分比来分析比较报表中相关项目的增减情况。最近一期的报表上的每个项目数据与前一期、前几期相同项目的金额相比较，同时列示每个项目的增减金额与增减百分比。水平分析可以用于对两个报表的比较，在这种情况下，以最早期间的报表和数据为基础，同各期报表相比较，进行分

pare historical data, such as ratios, or line items, over a number of accounting periods. Horizontal analysis takes into account either absolute comparison or percentage comparison, where the baseline amount is presented as 100%, while the amount in succeeding periods is presented as a percentage of that in the baseline year. Some analysts may call it as baseline analysis.

析。此外，也可以把每个报表与当期报表进行比较。

Horizontal analysis is used to review one company's financial statements over multiple periods. It is also usually described as a percentage growth over the same line item in the base year. Financial statements users always use horizontal analysis to discover trends and growth patterns of certain entities. A detail you need to know is that the ratio can be manipulated to make the current period look outstanding if specific historical periods of poor performance are chosen as a comparison, so that the growth rate can be relatively high in such situations.

Generally accepted accounting principles (GAAP) are based on consistency and comparability of financial statements. Consistency is the ability to accurately review one company's financial statements over a period of time because accounting methods and applications remain constant. Comparability is the ability to review side-by-side two or more different companies' financials. Horizontal analysis not only improves the review of a company's consistency over time directly, but also improves comparability of growth in a company to that of its competitors as well.

Horizontal analysis provides analysts a way to spot the factors driving the company's financial performance over time, as well as to find out trends and growth patterns such as seasonality. It enables analysts to assess relative changes in different line items over time, and project them into the future, which means future performance can be predicted based on current analysis. By looking at the income statement, balance sheet, and cash flow statement over time, one can create a complete picture of operational results, and see what has been driving a company's performance and whether it is operating efficiently and profitably.

Financial statements users can use performance ratios of business performance, such as profit margins, inventory turnover, and return on equity, to detect emerging problems and weaknesses, strengths and opportunities. For example, earnings per share (EPS) may have been rising because the cost of goods sold (COGS) have been falling, or because sales have been growing strongly. And coverage ratios, like the cash flow-to-debt ratio and the interest coverage ratio can be taken to reveal whether a company can service its debt through sufficient liquidity. Horizontal analysis also makes it easier to compare growth rates and profitability among multiple companies.

earnings per share (EPS) 每股收益

9.3 Ratio Analysis

Ratio analysis is a quantitative method of thoroughly examining into a company's liquidity, solvency, operational efficiency, and profitability by comparing information contained in its financial statements. Ratio analysis can be considered as a foundation of financial analysis. Both outsiders and insiders are potential users of financial statements. Outside analysts use different ratios to assess companies, while corporate insiders may rely on them to conclude financial decisions.

What does ratio analysis tell you? When investors and analysts talk about fundamental or quantitative analysis, they are usually referring to ratio analysis. Ratio analysis considers current and historical data within one company, with its peers through industries, so as to evaluate the company's financial performance and health.

Comparing a company's data of different financial period helps to assess whether the company is improving or deteriorating, comparing those with industry average can show a company's financial standing in the industry, and comparing a company to one or more other companies operating in its sector can help to see how the company

ratio analysis 比率分析法。通过计算多种比率，可对企业财务的流动能力、营运能力、盈利能力等进行量化分析。我们计算比率后可以与其他会计期间或者其他公司的数据进行对比，从而评估公司的相关情况。注意：比率一定要进行对比才有效；对单个比率的描述判断通常是没有意义的。利用比率分析法可对不同指标进行计算，与不同期数据或同行业不同企业数据进行比较，评价企业的各种财务状况和能力。

stacks up.

Ratio analysis can be used to establish a trend line for one company's results over a large number of financial reporting periods. Simply computing ratios within one period does not make any sense.

Comparing a company to its peers or its industry averages is another useful application for ratio analysis. Calculating one ratio for competitors in a given industry and comparing across the set of companies can reveal both positive and negative information.

Theoretically, since companies in the same industry typically have similar capital structures and business nature, their ratios might be relatively the same. However, ratios usually vary from one company to another even within the same industry. Different ratio results could mean that one firm has underlying issues, making them less competitive, and they could also mean that a certain company has much more robust potentials than its competitors. Many analysts use ratios to review sectors, looking for the most and least valuable companies in the group.

It should be noticed that:

—Ratio analysis compares line-item data from a company's financial statements to reveal insights regarding profitability, liquidity, operational efficiency, and solvency.

—Ratio analysis can be used to study trends over time for one company or to compare companies within an industry or sector.

—While ratios offer several types of insight, other types of information and analysis are usually needed to form a hologram of a company's financial position.

There are different types of ratios; most investors are familiar with a few key ratios. Frequently used ratios include the current ratio, return on capital employed (ROCE), the debt-equity (D/E) ratio, the dividend payout ratio, and the price/earnings (P/E) ratio, etc. While there are numerous financial ratios, they can be categorized into six main groups based on the types of information they provide. The six categories are Liquidity Ratio, Solvency Ratio,

Profitability Ratio, Efficiency Ratio, Coverage Ratio and Market Prospect Ratio. In the following part of this chapter, we shall introduce these categories of ratios respectively.

9.3.1 Liquidity Ratios

Liquidity ratios are an important class of financial metrics used to determine a debtor's ability to pay off current debt obligations without raising external capital. Liquidity ratios measure a company's ability to pay debt obligations. The metrics we usually use are the current ratio, quick ratio, and operating cash flow ratio.

It considers the current liabilities and liquid assets, as to assess the coverage of short-term debts in an emergency.

A few key points we should know about are:

▶ Liquidity ratios are an important class of financial metrics used to determine a debtor's ability to pay off current debt obligations without raising external capital.

▶ Common liquidity ratios include the quick ratio, current ratio, and days sales outstanding.

▶ Liquidity ratios determine a company's ability to cover short-term obligations.

What dose liquidity tell us?

Liquidity is the ability to quickly convert assets into cash at relatively low cost. These ratios can be used by both inside and outside analysts, and they are mostly useful when they are used in a comparative form.

Internal analysis regarding liquidity ratios assesses financial data from different financial periods with the same accounting policy.

Comparing the data of previous time periods to those of current time periods allows analysts to track changes in the business over time. In general, a higher liquidity ratio shows a company is more liquid and has better coverage of outstanding debts.

Alternatively, external analysis focuses on comparing the liquidity ratios of one company to another or an entire industry. This information

liquidity ratio 流动比率。流动比率用来衡量企业在不用对外发行股票的前提下偿还其流动负债的能力。

◎企业流动性分析可以做外部分析，也可以做内部分析。

◎内部分析关注同一企业、同一会计口径下比率在不同会计期间的变化情况，借此分析企业流动性的变化情况。

◎外部分析关注该企业与同行业某一企业或多个企业之间的差异。在同业中设立基准，并向其靠拢。

current ratio 流动比率。流动比率用以衡量企业用其流动资产覆盖其流动负债的能力。通常情况下，认为企业该指标与行业平均数持平或稍

is useful to evaluate the company's strategic positioning with its competitors as the best of the peers can be set as a benchmark to follow. Liquidity ratio analysis may be less effective when used across industries as different industries always come with different nature and business structures. Also, even within the same industry, liquidity ratio analysis is less effective for comparing businesses of different sizes, in different geographical locations, and with different risk appetites.

Common liquidity ratios we will introduce are Current Ratio, Quick Ratio and Days Sales Outstanding (DSO).

Current Ratio

The current ratio measures a company's ability to pay off its current liabilities with its current assets such as cash, accounts receivable and inventories. The ratio is computed by dividing the total current assets by the total current liabilities. Normally, the current ratio is considered acceptable if it is in accordance with or slightly higher than the industry average. Too high the current ratio may assume insufficient use of current assets, while one that is lower than the industry average could indicate higher risk of distress or default as it lacks the ability to pay off its debts.

$$\text{Current Ratio} = \frac{\text{Current Assets}}{\text{Current Liabilities}}$$

Quick Ratio

The quick ratio measures a company's ability to meet its short-term obligations with its most liquid assets and therefore excludes inventories from its current assets. It tests a company's ability to pay off its short-term obligation with its near-cash assets, the assets that can be quickly converted to cash, so that we should remove the inventory part from it as inventories sometimes take slightly longer to be converted into cash. It is also known as the "acid-test ratio":

$$\text{Quick Ratio} = \frac{C+MS+AR}{CL}$$

Where:

C = cash & cash equivalents, MS = marketable securities, AR =

微高于行业平均数较为合理。该指标过高可能意味流动资产囤积导致利用率不高；指标过低可能代表企业没有足够流动资产偿清流动负债。

quick ratio 速动比率。计算速动比率时考虑的是企业能够用快速变现的流动资产偿还流动负债的能力。所以对于存货，可能没有办法即刻将其变现，应该从分子中剔除。

days sales outstanding 应收账款周转天数。应收账款周转天数衡量的是企业收回赊销款项所花费的平均天数。

◎企业若能越快地将款项收回，则可更快地把资金投入生产销售中，从而提高收入。

accounts receivable, CL = current liabilities

Also, another way to express this equation is:

Days Sales Outstanding (***DSO***)

DSO refers to the average number of days it takes a company to collect payment after it makes a credit sale. A higher DSO means that a company is taking relatively longer period to collect payment from credit sales. DSOs are generally calculated on a monthly, quarterly or annually basis.

Companies tend to collect their outstanding receivables as quickly as possible because they can as soon return the money back to sales, thus generate more revenue.

A high DSO indicates the company makes sales to their customers, taking longer time to collect the money in cash form, while a low DSO shows the company takes less time to collect the money from credit sales. It should be noted that the DSO numbers vary from industry to industry, where the real estate industry comes with higher DSO and catering industry comes with lower one. Therefore, we usually compare DSO numbers of companies within a same industry.

$$DSO = \frac{\text{Average Account Receivable}}{\text{Revenue Per Day}}$$

Liquidity Crisis

A liquidity crisis can arise even at healthy companies if circumstances arise that make it difficult for them to meet short-term obligations such as repaying their loans and paying their employees. The global credit crunch of 2007-2008 is a typical example of liquidity catastrophe as most of us should know. The short-term debt of commercial papers issued by large companies to finance current assets and pay off current liabilities, plays a critical role in this financial crisis.

A near-total freeze in the $2 trillion U. S. commercial paper market made it exceedingly difficult for even the most solvent companies to raise short-term funds at that time and hastened the bankruptcy of giant corporations such as Lehman Brothers and General Motors Company.

◎不同行业根据其特性不同，应收账款收回天数会呈现较大差异，所以分析时最好选择同行业企业。

credit crunch 信贷危机
pledge 抵押
circumstances 条件；环境
short-term obligations 短期义务
financial crisis 金融危机
financial system 金融系统

But unless the financial system is in a credit crunch, a company-specific liquidity crisis can be resolved relatively easily with a liquidity injection, if the company is solvent. This is because the company can pledge some assets if required to raise cash to tide over the liquidity squeeze. This route may not be available for a company that is technically insolvent since a liquidity crisis would exacerbate its financial situation and force it into bankruptcy.

Let's use an example to demonstrate how these liquidity ratios can be considered to assess a company's financial condition.

Consider there are two companies－Louis Inc. and Sofie Co. － with the following assets and liabilities on their balance sheets (figures in millions of dollars). We assume that both companies operate in the same manufacturing sector (i. e., industrial glues and solvents).

Items	Louis Inc.	Sofie Co.
Cash/ $ million	5	1
Marketable Securities/ $ million	5	2
Accounts Receivable/ $ million	10	2
Inventories/ $ million	10	5
Current Assets (a) / $ million	30	10
Plant and Equipment (b) / $ million	25	65
Intangible Assets (c) / $ million	20	0
Total Assets ($a+b+c$) / $ million	75	75
Current Liabilities (d) / $ million	10	25
Long-Term Debt (e) / $ million	50	10
Total Liabilities (d+e) / $ million	60	35
Shareholders' Equity/ $ million	15	40
Ratios		
Current Ratio	3. 0	0. 40
Quick Ratio	2. 0	0. 20

Louis Inc. witnesses a high degree of liquidity. Its current ratio

assume 假设

manufacturing sector 制造业行业

witness 见证

solvency ratio 偿债能力比率。偿债能力比率用以衡量企业使用其现金流偿还长期负债的能力，是用来评价债权人保障程度的重要指标。

assumes it has 3 dollars of current assets to cover every dollar of current liabilities. Its quick ratio also indicates adequate liquidity even after excluding the amounts of inventories, which means 2 dollars in assets can be converted rapidly to cash to pay off every dollar of current liabilities.

Sofie's situation is quite different. The company has a current ratio of 0.4, which indicates an inadequate degree of liquidity with only 40 cents of current assets available to cover every \$1 of current liabilities. The quick ratio suggests an even more serious liquidity position, with only 20 cents of liquid assets for every \$1 of current liabilities.

If these two companies are within the same industry, Louis should be considered to have better liquidity ability than Sofie.

9.3.2 Solvency Ratios

The solvency ratio is usually used by potential business lenders to measure a company's ability to meet its total debt obligations. The solvency ratio indicates whether a company's cash flow is sufficient to meet both its short-term and long-term liabilities. It helps the analysts to determine how well the creditors are protected, and where there are the circumstances of bankruptcy. Usually the lower a company's solvency ratio, the greater the probability that it will default on its debt obligations.

Key points we should notice are:

▶ The solvency ratio examines a company's ability to meet its debt obligations from a long-term perspective.

▶ This ratio is most often used by prospective lenders to evaluate the worthiness of lending.

▶ A higher ratio usually indicates a company's greater ability to cover its liabilities over a long term.

The formula for the solvency ratio is shown as:

$$\text{Solvency Ratio} = \frac{\text{Net After-Tax Income} + \text{Non-cash Expenses}}{\text{Short-Term Liabilities} + \text{Long-Term Liabilities}}$$

◎计算偿债能力比率时用税后收入除以短期负债与长期负债的和，这里的分子应当加回非现金支出，比如折旧和摊销费用，因为这些项目虽然在利润表中列示，但却没有带来实际的现金流出。

The solvency ratio is calculated by dividing a company's after-tax net operating income by its total debt obligations. Non-cash expenses, such as depreciation and amortization should be added back to net income, to derive net after-tax income. The non-cash expenses are included in the income statement on accrual basis, but they do not involve any actual expense, so that they should be added back. These numerator figures come from the company's income statement.

Short-term and long-term liabilities are found on the company's balance sheet.

Then, what can we tell from calculating the solvency ratio? The solvency ratio is one of many metrics used to determine whether a company can stay solvent. Other solvency ratios include debt-to-equity, total-debt-to-total-assets, and interest coverage ratios.

The solvency ratio is a comprehensive measure of solvency, as it focuses on a firm's actual cash flow instead of just looking at the net income, as non-cash expenses are added back in calculation. It measures this cash flow capacity in relation to all liabilities, rather than only in short-term debt. This way, the solvency ratio assesses a company's ability to cover its debt obligations with real cash flow in a long-term perspective.

As a rule of thumb, a solvency ratio that is higher than 20% is financially safe, while those below the percentage may reveal potential risk; however, solvency ratios vary from industry to industry. A company's solvency ratio should, therefore, be compared with its competitors in the same industry rather than through any other industry or viewed in isolation.

Companies in debt-heavy industries like utilities and pipelines may have lower solvency ratios than those in sectors such as technology. To make an apples-to-apples comparison, the solvency ratio should be compared for companies in the same industry, to get a true picture of relative solvency.

Let's look at the solvency ratios for Mason Co. and Lemon Co. for the fiscal year ended Dec. 31, 2018.

after-tax net operating income 税后净经营收入

numerator 分子（数）

metrics 度量

debt-to-equity 负债权益比

interest coverage ratio 利息保障比率

Items	Mason	Lemon
Net Income/ $	2, 737	14, 293
Depreciation/ $	2, 298	10, 080
Net Income + Depreciation (A) / $	5, 035	24, 373
Short-Term Debt/ $	12, 708	66, 928
Long-Term Debt/ $	11, 031	36, 015
ST Debt + LT Debt (B) / $	23, 739	102, 943
Solvency Ratio = (A/B) /%	21. 21	23. 68

Both Mason and Lemon have solid solvency ratios lying above 20%. This means that they can close out their long-term debt obligations when they come due using operating income. Lenders looking through a company's financial statement will usually use the solvency ratio as a determinant for creditworthiness.

Measuring cash flow rather than net income is a better determinant of solvency, especially for the companies that incur large amounts of depreciation on their assets but have low levels of actual profitability.

profitability ratio 盈利能力比率。盈利能力比率指标用以评估企业创造利润的能力，衡量使用现有资产创造最大股东收益的能力。通常该比率越高，越能吸引投资者。但是对该指标的分析不仅要与同行业对比，还要关注该企业的历史数据以及盈利能力是否具有上升趋势和潜力。

9. 3. 3 Profitability Ratios

Profitability ratios are a class of financial metrics that are used to assess a business's ability to generate earnings relative to its revenue, operating costs, balance sheet assets, and shareholders' equity over time, using data from a specific point in time.

It is important to remark that:

▶ Profitability ratios show how well companies use their existing assets to generate profit and value for shareholders.

▶ Higher ratio results are often more favorable, but ratios provide much more information when compared to results from tother similar companies, the company's own historical performance, or the industry average numbers.

What can we find out from the profitability ratio? For most profitability ratios, having a higher value relative to a competitor's ratio or relative to the same ratio from a previous period indicates that the company is doing well. It indicates that one company is doing better than the other, or it performs better than previous periods and has certain potentials in the future. Ratios are most effective when used in a comparative form, to compare with similar companies, the company's own history, or average ratios for the company's industry average numbers.

◎不同行业可能面临不同特征的盈利变化；同一行业的企业可能也面临季节性特征的变化。

margin ratio 利润比率

return ratio 回报比率

profit margin 利润率

For example, gross profit margin is one of the most often-used profitable or margin ratios. Some industries experience seasonality in their operations, such as the retail industry. Retailers typically experience significantly higher revenues and earnings during holidays such as Christmas, Boxing Day and Black Friday. It would not make sense to compare a retailer's last quarter gross profit margin with its first quarter gross profit margin because the year-end quarter experiences more longer holidays and sales period, so that it would not reveal directly comparable information. Alternatively, comparing a retailer's last quarter or full-year profit margin with that from the same period in previous years would be more informative.

◎基于不同层次的费用扣除，我们可以得到不同种类的利润率，如毛利率、营业毛利率、税前利率、净利率。

Profitability ratios are the most popular metrics used in financial analysis, and they generally fall into two categories: margin ratios and return ratios. Margin ratios give insight, from several different angles, on a company's ability to turn sales into profit. Return ratios offer several different ways to examine how well a company generates a return for its shareholders. Some examples of profitability ratios are profit margin, return on assets (ROA), return on equity (ROE) and return on capital employed (ROCE). We will introduce those ratios correspondently.

◎根据费用扣减层次的逐渐增加，利润率会呈逐渐下降趋势（因为在分母不变的情况下，分子减小了）。

Margin Ratios: Profit Margin

Different profit margins are used to measure a company's profitability at disparate cost levels, including gross margin, operating margin, pretax margin, and net profit margin. The margins narrow down as different layers of additional costs are taken into consideration, such as the cost of goods sold (COGS), operating

◎企业所有者、管理者和咨询师可以通过分析利润率，了解企业全年的盈利变化规律，判断企业是否存在费用管理问题或销售问题，或者

and non-operating expenses, and taxes paid. It represents what percentage of sales has turned into profits. The percentage figure indicates how many cents of profit the business has generated for each dollar of sale. For instance, if a business reports that it achieved a 35% profit margin during the last quarter, it means that it had a net income of 35 cents for each dollar of sales generated.

There are several types of profit margin. The gross margin measures how much a company can mark up sales above COGS. The operating margin is the percentage of sales left after covering additional operating expenses. The pretax margin shows a company's profitability after further accounting for non-operating expenses. The net profit margin concerns a company's ability to generate earnings after taxes. In everyday use, however, it usually refers to net profit margin, a company's bottom line after all other expenses, including taxes and one-off oddities, have been taken out of revenue.

Let's see how these margins are properly calculated:

$$\text{Gross Profit Margin} = \frac{\text{Net Sales} - \text{Cost of Goods Sold}}{\text{Net Sales}}$$

$$\text{Operating Profit Margin} = \frac{\text{Operating Income}}{\text{Revenue}}$$

$$\text{Net Profit Margin} = \frac{\text{Net Income}}{\text{Revenue}}$$

Where net income is the revenue net of cost of goods sold, operating expenses, other expenses, interests and taxes.

From a billion-dollar publicly listed company to a random sidewalk sandwich stand, the profit margin ratio is widely used and quoted by all kinds of businesses across the globe. Beyond individual businesses, it is also used to indicate the profitability potential of larger sectors and of overall national or regional markets. The profit margin has become the globally adopted standard measure of the profit-generating capacity of a business and analysts can assess one company's potential by studying on this indicator. It is one of the first few key figures to be quoted in the quarterly result reports that compa-

深入分析有无存货积压和资源利用不善的情况。

◎外部投资者可以通过评估利润率指标来做出投资决策。

gross margin 毛利率
operating margin 营业利润率
net profit margin 净利润率
seasonal patterns 季节变化趋势
corporate performance 公司业绩

nies issue.

Internally, business owners, company management, and external consultants use it to encounter operational issues and to study seasonal patterns and corporate performance during different periods. A zero or negative profit margin translates to a business either having difficulties to achieve decent sales or failing to manage their cost well. Analyzing the ratio can help internal users dig further, like high level of unsold inventory, excess employees and underutilized resources, or high rentals, and then they may come up with appropriate action plans. Enterprises that operate multiple business divisions, product lines, stores, or geographically spread-out facilities may use profit margin to evaluate and compare the performance of each unit, to decide which unit should be reserved and which should not.

Profit margins often provide persuasive information when a company seeks funding. Individual businesses, like a local retail store, may need to provide financial statements with healthy profit margin ratio, to get loan from banks and other lenders. Large corporations issuing debt or equity financing are required to express their purpose and intention of using the money they are collecting, because that provides investors the company's ability of achieving expected profit margin, either by cutting costs or by increasing sales, or a combination of both ways. The ratios have also become an integral part of equity valuations in the primary market for initial public offerings (IPO).

Finally, profit margins are crucial for investors seeking to fund a more potentially profitable product or service. They may predict the future cash inflow of each product or service, and calculate the NPVs and relative margin ratios, then they can make decision on investing on a better one with considerable profit margin.

We'll look at some examples to see that the margin ratios of different companies vary from industry to industry.

Businesses of luxury goods and high-end accessories often operate on low sales but high profit potentials. Few costly items, like

excess employees 过剩员工
underutilized resources 未尽其用的资源
get loan from banks 从银行取得贷款
equity financing 权益融资
initial public offerings (IPO) 首次公开发行股票
future cash inflow 未来现金流
net present value (NPV) 净现值

software 软件
laptop 笔记本电脑
operation-intensive business 经营密集型企业

a luxury car, are ordered to build-that is, the unit is manufactured after securing the order from the customer, making it a low-expense process without much operational overheads.

Software or gaming companies may invest initially while developing a software/game and cash in big later by simply selling millions of copies with very little expenses. Getting into strategic agreements with device manufacturers, like offering pre-installed Windows and MS Office on Dell-manufactured laptops, further reduces the costs while maintaining revenues.

Operation-intensive businesses like transportation which may have to deal with fluctuating fuel prices, drivers' perks and retention, and vehicle maintenance usually have lower profit margins.

Agriculture-based ventures usually have low profit margins owing to weather uncertainty, high inventory, operational overheads, and need for farming and storage space, and resource-intensive activities.

Automobiles also have low profit margins, as profits and sales are limited by intense competition, uncertain consumer demand, and high operational expenses involved in developing dealership networks and logistics.

Patent-secured businesses like pharmaceuticals may incur high research costs initially, but they reap big with high profit margins while selling the patent-protected drugs with no competition.

The above cases may help understand this ratio better and rationally.

***Return Ratios*: *Return on Assets* (*ROA*)**

Return on assets (ROA) indicates how profitable a company can be in relation to its total assets. The ratio gives a manager, investor, or analyst an idea as to how efficient a company generates earnings with the total of its assets.

Profitability is assessed by considering revenue along with costs and expenses, and it is analyzed in comparison to assets to see how effective a company is in utilizing assets to generate sales and eventually result in profits. The term "return" in the ROA ratio refers to

fluctuating 浮动的

perks and retention 津贴及滞留

vehicle maintenance 车辆维修

agriculture-based venture 以农业为基础的企业

weather uncertainty 天气不确定性

overhead 运营费用；制造费用

resource-intensive 资源密集型

logistics 物流

pharmaceuticals 药品

patent-protected drugs 专利保护药品

◎通常企业拥有的资产越多，创造利益的潜力越大。因为规模经济可以降低单位成本，从而提高收益率。

ROA 资产报酬率。资产报酬率用以衡量企业使用其资产创造收益的能力。

net profit or net income, which is the amount of earnings from sales deducting all costs, expenses, and taxes.

Typically, the more assets a company has acquired, the more sales and potentially more profits the company may generate. As economies of scale help lower costs and improve margins, returns may grow at a faster rate than assets, ultimately increasing return on assets.

ROA is calculated by dividing a company's net income by total assets. The formula would be expressed as:

$$ROA = \frac{\text{Net Income}}{\text{Total Assets}}$$

Higher ROA indicates more efficient use of assets.

We can illustrate the analysis of ROA through an example. Suppose Sam and Fran both start hot dog stands. Sam spends \$1,500 on a bare-bone metal cart, while Fran spends \$15,000 on a zombie apocalypse-themed unit, complete with costume. Let's assume that those were the only assets each deployed. If over some given time period Sam has earned \$150 and Fran has earned \$1,200, Fran would have the more valuable business, but Sam would have the more efficient one. Using the above formula, we see Sam's simplified ROA is \$150/\$1,500 = 10%, while Fran's simplified ROA is \$1,200/\$15,000 = 8%. While Sam earns less than Fran, the former has higher ROA than the latter. We cannot make judgement by focusing merely on the absolute earnings, instead we need to see the whole picture.

Return on assets (ROA) basically tells you how much earnings can be generated from assets. It is also important to know that the ratio varies from industry to industry, which is why ROA is always used in a comparative form. It is evident to compare that against a company's previous ROA numbers or against that in a similar company. Normally speaking, the higher the ROA number, the better, because the company is assessed as earning more money on less investment.

◎ROA 用以衡量企业使用资产创造收益的效率。通常 ROA 越高越好，说明企业可以用经济的资源创造更多的财富。

◎我们知道，“资产 = 负债 + 所有者权益”，那么 ROA 分母的数据就应该是债务和债券融资的总和。部分学者认为融资成本也应该包括在计算 ROA 的过程中，所以应在分母加上相关融资成本和利息费用的金额。

Remember total assets are also the sum of its total liabilities and shareholder's equity. Both types of financing are used to fund the operations of the company. Since a company's assets are either funded by debt or equity, some analysts and investors suppose the cost of acquiring the assets should also be considered, thus adding back interest expense in the formula for ROA calculation.

denominator 分母（数）
e-commerce 电子商务

In other words, the impact of taking more debt is negated by adding back the cost of borrowing to the net income and using the average assets in each period as the denominator. Interest expense is added because the net income amount on the income statement excludes interest expense.

ROA is most useful for comparing companies in the same industry, as different industries use assets differently. For example, the ROA for service-oriented firms, such as banks, will be significantly higher than the ROA for capital intensive companies, such as construction or utility companies.

Let's evaluate the return on assets (ROA) for three companies in the retail industry: Macy's, Kohl's and Dillard's.

The data and ratios are shown as:

Company	Net Income/ $ billion	Total Assets/ $ billion	ROA/%
Macy's	1.7	20.4	8.3
Kohl's	0.996	14.1	7.1
Dillard's	0.243	3.9	6.2

ROE 净资产收益率，又称股权收益率。ROE 反映投资人股权创造价值的能力。因为“权益=资产-负债”，所以 ROE 通常称为净资产收益率。

Due to the increasing popularity of e-commerce, brick and mortar retail companies have taken a hit in the level of profits they generate using their available assets. Still, every dollar that Macy's has invested in assets generates 8.3 cents of net income. Macy's is better at converting its investment into profits, compared with Kohl's and Dillard's. One of management's most important jobs is to make wise choices in allocating its resources, and it appears that Macy's management is more adept than its two peers.

***Return Ratios*: *Return on Equity* (*ROE*)**

ROE is a ratio that concerns a company's equity holders the most since it measures their ability to earn a return on their equity investments. Because shareholders' equity is equal to a company's assets minus its debt, ROE could be thought of as the return on net assets. ROE may increase dramatically without any equity addition when it can simply benefit from a higher return helped by a larger asset base. As a company increases its asset size and generates a better return with higher margins, equity holders can retain much of the return growth when additional assets are the result of debt use.

ROE is expressed as a percentage and can be calculated for any company if net income and equity are both positive numbers. Net income is calculated before dividends are paid to common shareholders and after dividends to preferred shareholders and interest to lenders, as dividends paid to preferred shareholders are always guaranteed by contracts.

◎计算净利润时，应当扣除优先股股利和债权人利息，不扣除普通股股利。

$$ROE = \frac{\text{Net Income}}{\text{Average Shareholders' Equity}}$$

Net Income is the amount of income net of expense, and taxes that a company generates for a given period. Average Shareholders' Equity is calculated based on equity at the beginning and the end of the period. The amount of net income over the last full fiscal year, or trailing 12 months, is found on the income statement. The amount of shareholders' equity comes from the balance sheet.

◎计算 ROE 时应与同行业进行对比。若该指标与同业平均值持平或略高于同业平均值，则认为该企业净资产回报率指标较好。

Return on equity (ROE) is deemed useful when compared with that of the peers since the ratios in different industries are quite different. For example, a normal ROE in the utility sector could be 10% or less, while a technology or retail firm with smaller balance sheet accounts relative to net income may have normal ROE levels of 18% or more.

ROCE 已占用资本回报率。该指标用以评估企业使用其已占用资本创造价值的能力。

A good rule of thumb is to target an ROE that is equal to or just above the average for the peer group. For example, assume a company, Tech Co, has maintained a steady ROE of 18% over the last few years compared to the average of its peers, which was 15%. An investor could conclude that Tech Co's management is above average at

EBIT 息税前利润（=收入-成本-营业费用）

using the company's assets to create profits.

Relatively high or low ROE ratios will vary significantly from one industry group or sector to another. When used to evaluate one company to another similar company the comparison will be more meaningful. A common shortcut for investors to consider a return on equity near the long-term average of the S&P 500（14%）as an acceptable ratio and anything less than 10% as poor.

Both ROA and ROE are measures of how a company utilizes its resources. Essentially, ROE only measures the return on a company's equity, leaving out the liabilities. Thus, ROA accounts for a company's debt and ROE does not. The more leverage and debt a company takes on, the higher ROE will be when compared to ROA.

***Return Ratios: Return on Capital Employed*（*ROCE*）**

Return on capital employed（ROCE）is a financial ratio that measures one company's profitability and efficiency with the capital owned by this company. It indicates how well the entity can generate profits with its own capital. It is a primary ratio usually considered by investors when seeking potential investing candidates. There is not merely one method to calculate ROCE. As the results can be used for comparative purposes, the same method of calculation is used over time.

The formula for ROCE is illustrated as:

$$ROCE = \frac{EBIT}{Capital\ Employed}$$

Where:

EBIT = Earnings Before Interests and Tax

Capital Employed = Total Assets - Current Liabilities

Earnings before interest and tax（EBIT）, also known as operating income, shows how much a company earns from its operations alone without considering interests or taxes. EBIT is calculated by subtracting the cost of goods sold and operating expenses from revenues.

Capital employed is the total amount of capital utilized by a company in order to generate profits. It is the sum of shareholders' equity

CE 企业所占有的资产（=股东权益+债务），计算时可以简化为：CE=总资产-流动负债

◎ROCE 更多用于评估资本密集型企业。相比 ROE 分析仅仅关注了企业的权益，ROCE 关注的是企业的权益和债务的总和。对于负债较高的行业，对 ROCE 的分析显得更为合适。

◎在特殊情况下可以对计算做出调整，比如企业在短时间内持有大笔现金，但该现金并不能由该企业任意支配，计算时应当从所占有资本中扣除该笔现金的金额。

and debt liabilities. It also can be simply calculated as total assets minus current liabilities. Instead of using capital employed at an arbitrary point in time, analysts and investors often calculate ROCE based on the average capital employed, which takes the average of opening and closing capital employed for the period under analysis.

Average Capital Employed (CE) = (Opening CE + Closing CE) / 2

After we have introduced how this ratio is calculated, we need to figure out what this ratio tells us.

ROCE is especially useful when comparing the performance of companies in capital-intensive sectors such as utilities and telecoms. This is because unlike other fundamentals such as return on equity (ROE), which only analyzes profitability related to a company's common equity, ROCE considers debt and other liabilities as well. This provides a better indication of financial performance for companies with significant debt.

Adjustments may sometimes be required to get a truer depiction of ROCE. A company may occasionally have an inordinate amount of cash on hand, but since such cash is not actively employed in the business, it may need to be subtracted from the Capital Employed figure to get a more accurate measure of ROCE.

For a company, the ROCE trend over the years is also an important indicator of performance. In general, investors tend to favor companies with stable and rising ROCE numbers over companies where ROCE is volatile and bounces around from one year to the next.

9.3.4 Efficiency Ratios

The efficiency ratio is typically used to analyze how well a company uses its assets and liabilities internally. Efficiency ratios are taken to assess the turnover of receivables, the repayment of liabilities, the quantity and usage of equity, and the general use of inventory and machinery. This ratio can also be used to track and analyze the performance of commercial and investment banks.

efficiency ratio 效益比率。该指标用以评价企业有效使用其资产和负债创造利润的能力。

◎评价资产的有效利用率很重要，因为通常资产利用率高的企业能创造更多利润。

turnover of receivables 应收账款周转率

repayment of liabilities 偿还负债

maximize its wealth 最大化财富

improvement in the efficiency ratios 效率的提高

enhanced profitability 盈利能力的提升

Efficiency ratios, also known as activity ratios, are used by analysts to measure a company's short-term performance. The ratios mainly focus on a company's current assets or current liabilities, quantifying the operations of the business.

fixed asset turnover 固定资产周转率

An efficiency ratio measures a company's ability to use its assets to generate income and maximize its wealth. For example, an efficiency ratio often looks at various aspects of the company, such as the time it takes to collect cash from customers or the amount of time it takes to convert inventory to cash. This makes efficiency ratios analysis important, because an improvement in the efficiency ratios usually translates to enhanced profitability.

These ratios can be compared with peers in the same industry and can identify businesses that are better managed relative to the others. Some common efficiency ratios are accounts receivable turnover, fixed asset turnover, sales to inventory, sales to net working capital, accounts payable to sales and stock turnover ratio.

Inventory Turnover Ratio

inventory turnover ratio 存货周转率。通过计算存货周转率，可以推算企业的销售量是否足以推动存货的周转，同时也可以判断企业存货的储量是否存在过多或者过少的情况。存货周转率较低的企业可能存在销售问题或者存货管理的问题。分析该比率可以推测当前产品的销售前景或者存货是否存在积压的问题。该比率相对较高时表明企业可以更快地卖出存货。由此可推测可能是因为销售

The inventory turnover ratio measures a company's ability to manage its inventory efficiently and provides insight into the sales of a company. The ratio measures how many times the total average inventory has been sold over a certain period. Analysts use the ratio to determine if there are enough sales being generated to turn or utilize the inventory. The ratio also shows how well inventory is being managed including whether too much or not enough inventory is being bought.

The ratio is calculated by dividing the cost of goods sold by the average inventory.

$$\text{Inventory Turnover Ratio} = \frac{\text{Sales}}{\text{Average Inventory}}$$

Inventory turnover ratio tells us how fast the company can sell its inventory. The ratio can be recorded to compare with its own from different course of periods, or with its peers in the same industry within identical duration.

A low inventory turnover ratio implies weak sales and insufficient management of inventory. It may disclose problems in the sales part or unhealthy marketing situation. On the other hand, there may be constantly excess inventories, known as over-stocking.

策略好，市场前景好，或者存货管理方法先进。

On the contrary, a relevantly high inventory turnover ratio could suggest the inventory in stock can be sold quickly to get money back in business activities, due to possible good sales strategies, potentially prosperous marketing or sophisticated skills in inventory management.

For example, suppose Company A sold computers for \$5 million during the whole fiscal year. The average inventory of Company A is \$20 million. The inventory turnover ratio for the company is 0.25 (\$5 million/\$20 million). This indicates that Company A is not managing its inventory properly because it only sold a quarter of its inventory for the year.

Asset Turnover Ratio

The asset turnover ratio measures a company's ability to efficiently generate revenues from its assets. In other words, the asset turnover ratio calculates sales as a percentage of the company's assets. The ratio is effective in showing how many sales are generated from each dollar of assets a company owns.

asset turnover ratio 资产周转率。资产周转率用以衡量企业使用自己的资产有效创造收益的能力。使用该比率可测算一个特定会计期间每一元钱的资产能够创造多少收入。相对较高的资产周转率表明企业使用资产创造价值的效率较高，资产周转率相对较低时表明企业使用资产创造价值的效率较低。

A higher asset turnover ratio means the company's management is using its assets more efficiently, while a lower ratio means the company's management isn't using its assets efficiently.

The ratio is calculated by dividing a company's revenues by its total assets.

$$\text{Assets Turnover Ratio} = \frac{\text{Revenue}}{\text{Total Assets}}$$

For example, suppose a company has total assets of \$1,000,000 and sales or revenue of \$300,000 for the period. The asset turnover ratio would equal 0.30 (\$300,000/\$1,000,000). In other words, the company generates 30 cents for every dollar in assets.

Receivables Turnover Ratio

The receivable turnover ratio measures how efficiently a company can actively collect its debts and extend its credits. The ratio is calculated by dividing a company's net credit sales by its average accounts receivable. It indicates how efficiently the company collects its short-term debts from credit sales.

$$\text{Receivable Turnover Ratio} = \frac{\text{Net Credit Sales}}{\text{Average Accounts Receivable}}$$

Normally, a high receivable turnover ratio suggests that a company can efficiently collets its money from credit sales. Analysts can predict that it has a high proportion of clients with quality credits, or the company is conservative when it comes to credit policy. Sometimes a good credit policy can help the company extend credits to quality customers, while avoiding approving credits to those who are not able to pay off on time.

Meanwhile, a low receivable turnover ratio implies the company is experiencing difficulties in collecting receivables. It may be caused by poor collection process or bad credit policy. In such circumstances, the entity should reassess its collection process and credit policy, to help activate its real cash inflow.

For example, a company has an average account receivable of $100,000, which is the result after averaging the beginning balance and ending balance of the account receivable balance for the period. The sales for the period were $300,000, so the receivable turnover ratio would equal 3, meaning the company collected its receivables three times for that period.

Typically, a company with a higher account receivable turnover ratio relative to its peers is favorable. A higher receivable turnover ratio indicates the company is more efficient than its competitors when collecting accounts receivable.

receivable turnover ratio 应收账款周转率。它用来评价企业收回其应收款项的效率。应收账款周转率较高时说明企业能够迅速地收回其赊销的应收款项。由此推测可能是因为企业信用政策较好、收款方法好或是客户信用评级高。该比率较低时，可能说明企业收款存在困难。企业信用政策可能过于宽松或者收款程序方法欠佳。

collecting receivables 回收应收账款

credit policy 信用政策

9.3.5 Coverage Ratios

A coverage ratio, broadly, is a group of measures of a company's ability to service its debt and meet its financial obligations such as interest or dividend payments. The higher the coverage ratio,

coverage ratio 保偿比率。保偿比率指标用以测算企业能够覆盖其负债、利息和支付股利的

the easier it should be to make interest payments on its debt or pay dividends. The trend of coverage ratios over time is also studied by analysts and investors to ascertain the change in a company's financial position.

能力。该类指标越高，暗示企业可以更好地满足债权人和股权人的投资回报。

Investors can use coverage ratios in one of two ways.

Firstly, you can track changes in the company's debt situation over time. In cases where the debt-service coverage ratio is barely within the acceptable range, it may be a good idea to look at the company's recent history. If the ratio has been gradually declining, it may only be a matter of time before it falls below the recommended figure.

◎投资人可以分析同一家企业不同会计期间保偿比率指标的变化情况，亦可在同行业中与其他企业进行比较。

Secondly, coverage ratios are also valuable when looking at a company in relation to its competitors. Evaluating similar businesses is imperative, because an interest coverage ratio acceptable in one industry may be considered risky in another field. If the business you're evaluating seems out of step with major competitors, it's often a red flag.

While comparing the coverage ratios of companies in the same industry or sector can provide valuable insights into their relative financial positions, doing so across companies in different sectors is not as useful, since it might be like to comparing apples and oranges.

Common coverage ratios include the interest coverage ratio, the debt service coverage ratio, the asset coverage ratio and other coverage ratio. They will be introduced in the following part.

Interest Coverage Ratio

Interest coverage ratio 利息保偿率。用以衡量企业使用息税前利润偿还债务利息的能力。

The interest coverage ratio measures the ability of a company to pay the interest expense on its debt. The ratio, also known as the times interest, earned ratio, is defined as:

$$\text{Interest Coverage Ratio} = \frac{\text{EBIT}}{\text{Interest Expenses}}$$

Where: EBIT = Earnings Before Interests and Taxes

An interest coverage ratio of two or higher is generally considered satisfactory, as the company has enough funds to cover any interest expenses, thus, to prevent creditors' interests.

Debt Service Coverage Ratio

The debt service coverage ratio (DSCR) measures how well a company is able to pay its entire debt service. Debt service includes all principal and interest payments due to be made in the near term. The ratio is defined as:

$$DSCR=\frac{\text{Net Operating Income}}{\text{Total Debt Service}}$$

Where:

Net Operating Income = Revenue − Certain Operating Expenses

Total Debt Service = Current Debt Obligations

A ratio of one or above is indicative that a company generates sufficient earnings to completely cover its debt obligations.

Asset Coverage Ratio

The asset coverage ratio is similar in nature to the debt service coverage ratio but looks at balance sheet assets instead of comparing income to debt levels. The asset coverage ratio is a financial metric that measures how well a company can repay its debts by selling or liquidating its assets. The asset coverage ratio is important because it helps lenders, investors, and analysts measure the financial solvency of a company. Banks and creditors often look for a minimum asset coverage ratio before lending money, due to cautious principle. This ratio is defined as:

$$\text{Asset Coverage Ratio}=\frac{\text{Total Assets}-\text{Short-Term Liabilities}}{\text{Total Debt}}$$

Where Total Assets consist of tangibles, such as land, buildings, machinery and inventory.

As a rule of thumb, utilities should have an asset coverage ratio of at least 1.5, and industrial companies should have an asset coverage ratio of at least 2.

Other Coverage Ratios

Several other coverage ratios are also used by analysts, though they are not as usually used as the above three:

The fixed-charge coverage ratio measures a firm's ability to cover

debt service coverage ratioc (DSCR) 债务偿付比率。用以衡量企业使用净营业收入覆盖债务总额的能力。

debt obligation 负债义务

asset coverage ratio 资产偿付率。资产偿付率用来测算企业在变卖资产的情况下偿还负债的能力。

as a rule of thumb 根据经验；一般说来

fixed-charge coverage ratio 固定支出覆盖率

loan life coverage ratio (LLCR) 贷款保障比率

preferred dividend coverage ratio 优先股股利覆盖率

liquidity coverage ratio (LCR) 流动资金覆盖率

its fixed charges, such as debt payments, interest expense and equipment lease expense. It shows how well a company's earnings can cover its fixed expenses. Banks often look at this ratio when evaluating whether to lend money to a business.

The loan life coverage ratio (LLCR) is a financial ratio used to estimate the solvency of a firm, or the ability of a borrowing company to repay an outstanding loan. The LLCR is calculated by dividing the net present value (NPV) of the money available for debt repayment by the amount of outstanding debt.

The EBITDA-to-interest coverage ratio is a ratio that is used to assess a company's financial durability by examining whether it is at least profitable enough to pay off its interest expenses.

The preferred dividend coverage ratio is a coverage ratio that measures a company's ability to pay off its required preferred dividend payments. Preferred dividend payments are the scheduled dividend payments that are required to be paid on the company's preferred stock shares. Unlike common stock shares, the dividend payments for preferred stock are set in advance and cannot be changed from quarter to quarter. The company is required to pay them.

The liquidity coverage ratio (LCR) refers to the proportion of highly liquid assets held by financial institutions, to ensure their ongoing ability to meet short-term obligations. This ratio is essentially a generic stress test that aims to anticipate market-wide shocks and make sure that financial institutions possess suitable capital preservation, to ride out any short-term liquidity disruptions that may plague the market.

The capital loss coverage ratio is the difference between an asset's book value and the amount received from a sale relative to the value of the nonperforming assets being liquidated. The capital loss coverage ratio is an expression of how much transaction assistance is provided by a regulatory body in order to have an outside investor take part.

Sometimes we cannot make judgment according to a single ratio.

capital loss coverage ratio
资本损失率

Let's look at an example company, Leona Inc. The company generates a quarterly profit of \$200,000 (EBIT is \$300,000) and corresponding interest payments of \$50, 000. Leona did much of its borrowing during a period of low interest rates. Its interest coverage ratio looks extremely favorable:

Interest Coverage Ratio = \$300,000/\$50,000 = 6.0

The debt-service coverage ratio, however, reflects a significant principal amount the company pays each quarter totaling \$140,000. The resulting figure of 1.05 leaves little room for error if the company's sales take an unexpected hit:

DSCR = \$200,000/\$190,000 ≈ 1.05

Even though the company is generating a positive cash flow, it looks riskier from a debt perspective once debt-service coverage is taken into consideration.

market prospect ratio 市场前景指标。该类指标包括股息生息率、市盈率、每股收益、股息支付率等。通过测算此类指标，投资者可以得知相应的投资报酬率，并且预测股市的未来变化情况。

9.3.6 Market Prospect Ratios

These ratios are most commonly used in fundamental analysis and include dividend yield, P/E ratio, earnings per share, and dividend payout ratio. Investors use these ratios to determine what they may receive from their investments and to predict what the trend of a stock will be in the future, so that they can decide on investing potential companies.

Now, we will introduce those prominent ratios one after another.

Dividend Yield

dividend yield 股息生息率。它是一年的总派息额与当时市价的比率。

The dividend yield is the ratio of a company's annual dividend compared to its share price. The dividend yield is represented as a percentage and is calculated as follows:

$$\text{Dividend Yield} = \frac{\text{Annual Dividend}}{\text{Share Price}}$$

Generally, the annual dividend expressed in the calculation could be the total dividends paid during the most recent fiscal year, the total dividend paid over the past four quarters, or the most recent dividend multiplied by four.

The dividend yield is an estimate of the dividend return of a stock investment. Assuming the dividend is not raised or lowered, the yield will rise when the price of the stock falls, and it will fall when the price of the stock rises. Because dividend yields change with the stock price, it often looks unusually high for stocks that are falling quickly.

Because the dividend itself does not change frequently, the dividend yield always changes as share price changes. It will rise when the share price falls and decline when the share price rises. Some stock sectors, like consumer non-cyclical or utilities, will pay a higher dividend than average. Small or new companies that are still in growth stage will pay a lower dividend than mature companies in the same sectors.

Let's take a look at an example of dividend yield.

Suppose Company A's stock is trading at ＄20 and pays annual dividends of ＄1 per share to its shareholders. Also, suppose that Company B's stock is trading at ＄40 and also pays an annual dividend of ＄1 per share.

This means Company A's dividend yield is 5% （＄1 / ＄20）, while Company B's dividend yield is only 2.5% （＄1 / ＄40）. Assuming all other factors are equivalent, an investor looking to use their portfolio to supplement their income. The investor would likely prefer Company A over Company B, as it has double the dividend yield.

P/E Ratio

The price-to-earning ratio （P/E ratio） is the ratio for valuing a company that measures its current price per share relative to its per-share earnings （EPS）. The price-to-earning ratio is also sometimes known as the price multiple or the earnings multiple.

P/E ratios are used by investors and analysts to determine the relative value of a company's shares. It can also be used to compare a company against its own historical record or to compare against its peers over time.

P/E ratio 市盈率。市盈率是指股票价格除以每股收益（每股收益 EPS）的比率。

stock valuation 股票估值

overvalued or undervalued 高估或低估

S&P 500 Index 标准普尔 500 指数

$$P/E\ RATIO = \frac{Market\ Value\ Per\ Share}{Earnings\ Per\ Share}$$

The price-to-earnings ratio or P/E is one of the most widely used stock analysis tools used by investors and analysts for determining stock valuation. In addition to showing whether a company's stock price is overvalued or undervalued, the P/E can reveal how a stock's valuation compares to its industry group or a benchmark like the S&P 500 Index.

In essence, the P/E ratio also tells the investors the dollar amount they are expected to invest in a company in order to receive one dollar in return from that company. This is why the P/E is sometimes referred to as the price multiple because it shows how much investors are willing to pay per dollar of earnings. If a company was currently trading at a P/E multiple of 20x, the interpretation is that an investor is willing to pay \$20 for \$1 of current earnings.

If a company was currently trading at a P/E multiple of 20x, the interpretation is that an investor is willing to pay \$20 for \$1 of current earnings. 如果一家公司当前的股价是20倍的市盈率，可以理解为投资者愿意为当前1美元的收益支付20美元。

The P/E ratio helps investors determine the market value of a stock as compared to the company's earnings. In short, the P/E ratio shows what the market is willing to pay today for a stock based on its past or future earnings. A high P/E could mean that a stock's price is high relative to earnings and possibly overvalued. Conversely, a low P/E might indicate that the current stock price is low relative to earnings.

market value of a stock 一只股票的市值

shares outstanding 发行在外的股票

As a historical example, let's calculate the P/E ratio for Walmart Stores Inc. (WMT) as of November 14, 2017, when the company's stock price closed at \$91.09. The company's profit for the fiscal year ending January 31, 2017, was US \$13.64 billion, and its number of shares outstanding was 3.1 billion. Its EPS can be calculated as \$13.64 billion /3.1 billion = \$4.40.

Walmart's P/E ratio is, therefore, \$91.09 / \$4.40 = 20.70x.

Dividend Payout Ratio

The dividend payout ratio is the ratio of the total amount of dividends paid out to shareholders relative to the net income of the com-

dividend payout ratio 股息支付率。它是向股东分派的股息占公司盈利

pany. It is the percentage of earnings paid to shareholders in dividends. The amount that is not paid to shareholders is retained by the company to pay off debt or to reinvest in core operations. It is sometimes simply referred to as the "payout ratio".

The dividend payout ratio provides an indication of how much money a company is returning to shareholders versus how much it keeps on hand to reinvest in growth, pays off debt, or adds to cash reserves (retained earnings).

The dividend payout ratio can be calculated as the yearly dividend per share divided by the earnings per share, or equivalently, the dividends divided by net income (as shown below).

$$\text{Dividend Payout Ratio}=\frac{\text{Dividend Paid}}{\text{Net Income}}$$

On a per-share basis, the retention ratio can be expressed as:

$$\text{Retention Ratio}=\frac{\text{Dividend Per Share}}{\text{EPS}}$$

Alternatively, the dividend payout ratio can also be calculated as:

Dividend Payout = 1−Retention Ratio

Companies staying at different enterprise lifecycle may come up with different decision on dividend payout. A new, growth-oriented company that aims to expand, develop new products, and move into new markets would be expected to reinvest most or all of its earnings and could be understood for having a low or even zero payout ratio. The payout ratio is 0% for the companies that do not pay dividends.

On the other hand, a mature, established company that returns a little to shareholders would test investors' patience, because shareholders would not understand why the company payout does the dividend if it is not aiming to expand reinvestment. In 2012 and after nearly twenty years since its last dividend paying, Apple (AAPL) began to pay a dividend when the new CEO felt the company's enormous cash flow made a 0% payout ratio difficult to justify. Since it implies that a company has moved past its initial growth stage, a high

的百分比。该指标反映普通股股东从每股的全部净收益中分得多少，就单独的普通股投资者来讲，这一指标比每股净收益更直接体现当前利益。

◎公司所在的发展阶段很大程度上会影响其股息支付的比例。

◎处于成长期的公司需要利用留存收益进行大量投资和生产，故可能减少甚至暂时不分红。

◎成熟期的公司，已不需要大量投入资金了，所以可以增加分红比率。该比率也被报表使用者看作公司营运潜力和持续经营能力的有利指标。

payout ratio means share prices are unlikely to appreciate rapidly.

The payout ratio is also useful for assessing a dividend's sustainability. Companies are extremely reluctant to cut dividends since it can drive the stock price down and reflect poorly on management's abilities. If a company's payout ratio is over 100%, it is returning more money to shareholders than it is earning and will probably be forced to lower the dividend or stop paying it altogether. That result is not inevitable, however. A company endures a bad year without suspending payouts, and it is often in their interest to do so. It is therefore important to consider future earnings expectations and calculate a forward-looking payout ratio to contextualize the backward-looking one.

Long-term trends in the payout ratio also matter. A steadily rising ratio could indicate a healthy, maturing business, but a spiking one could mean the dividend is heading into unsustainable territory.

The retention ratio is a converse concept to the dividend payout ratio. The dividend payout ratio evaluates the percentage of profits earned that a company pays out to its shareholders.

Companies that make a profit at the end of a fiscal period can do a number of things with the profit they earned. They can pay it to shareholders as dividends, they can retain it to reinvest in the business for growth, or they can do both. The portion of the profit that a company chooses to pay out to its shareholders can be measured with the payout ratio.

For example, on November 29, 2017, The Walt Disney Company declared a $0.84 semi-annual cash dividend per share to shareholders of record December 11, to be paid January 11. As of the fiscal year ended September 30, 2017, the company's EPS was $5.73. Its retention ratio is, therefore, $0.84 / $5.73 = 0.1466, or 14.66%. Disney will pay out 14.66% and retain 85.34%.

sustainability 可持续性

forward-looking 远见的

long-term trends 长期趋势

retention ratio 留存比例

converse concepts 相反的概念

semi-annual 半年度的

Exercise 9

1. Ratio analysis for Aspect Co. (An extraction example from ACCA sample paper 2017)

Assume that you are the financial manager of Aspect Co. And you are just asked to report to the board about the financial performance of Aspect as the year ended 20×4. You should perform analysis on the company based on the financial statement information given below:

Statement of Financial Position as at Year Ended 20×4 unit: $ '000

Assets		
Non-current assets		24, 400
Current assets		
Inventory	4, 900	
Receivables	5, 700	
Cash at bank	2, 300	12, 900
Total assets		37, 300
Equity and liabilities		
Equity		
Equity shares		1, 000
Retained earnings		8, 000
		9, 000
Liabilities		
Non-current liabilities		
Loan		16, 700
Current liabilities		
Trade payables	5, 400	
Current tax payable	6, 200	11, 600
Total equity and liabilities		37, 300

Statement of Profit or Loss as of the Year Ended 20×4 unit: $ '000

Revenue	52, 100
Cost of sales	(20, 300)
Gross Profit	31, 800
Operating expenses	(12, 212)
Profit before tax	19, 588

Note (i)

	KPI
Gross profit margin/%	45
Operating profit margin/%	28
Receivables collection period/day	41
Current ratio	1. 6
Acid test (quick) ratio	1. 4
Gearing (debt/equity) /%	240

Requirements:

(a) Calculate the 20×4 ratios for Aspect Co.

(c) Using the ratios calculated in part (a), comment on Aspect Co's 20×4 performance and financial position compared to the industry average KPIs provided in note (i).

2. Ratio analysis for Gregory Co. (Extracted from ACCA sample exam 2016)

Gregory Co. is a listed company. As the chief financial manager, you are expected to analyze on its profitability and asset utilization during 20×5 and 20×6. Using the financial statements, calculate the following ratios for Gregory Co. for the years ended 31 March 20×6 and 20×5 and comment on the comparative performance:

(ⅰ) Return on capital employed (ROCE)

(ⅱ) Net asset turnover

(ⅲ) Gross profit margin

(ⅳ) Operating profit margin

The summarized financial statements of Gregory Co. on 31 March 20×5 and 31 March 20×6 are given:

Statement of financial position as at	31 March 20×6/ \$ '000	31 March 20×5/ \$ '000
Assets		
Non-current assets		
Property, plant and equipment	57,600	41,500
Current assets	44,000	36,000
Total assets	101,600	77,500
Equity and liabilities		
Equity		
Equity shares of \$ 1 each	46,000	40,000
Share premium	9,600	Nil
Retained earnings	18,700	13,000
	74,300	53,000
Current liabilities	27,300	24,500
Total equity and liabilities	101,600	77,500

Statement of profit or loss for the year ended	31 March 20×6/ \$ '000	31 March 20×5/ \$ '000
Revenue	46,500	28,000
Cost of sales	(37,200)	(20,800)
Gross profit	9,300	7,200
Operating expenses	(1,800)	(1,200)
Profit before tax (operating profit)	7,500	6,000
Income tax expense	(1,500)	(1,000)
Profit for the year	6,000	5,000

Appendix：Answers of Exercises 1 to 9

Exercise 1

1. （1） B；（2） C
2. （1） A profit-oriented organization means its main purpose is to seek profit through business activities.
   （2） Red Cross，CSR Europe，CCA （China Consumer Association） et al.
   （3） The term "limited liability" means that the owners of such companies are required to finance the business only up to an agreed amount. Once they have contributed the agreed amount，they cannot be called on to contribute any more，even if the company gets into financial difficulties.
   （4） A "sole trader" is a type of enterprise that is owned and run by one natural person and in which there is no legal distinction between the owner and the business entity. A partnership entity is very similar to a sole trader entity except that there must be at least two owners of the business.
   （5） The main characteristics of a company is that a company is a separate legal entity，and it has limited liability.

Exercise 2

1. a） liability （负债）； b） revenue （收入）； c） asset （资产）； d） expense （费用）； e） equity （所有者权益）
2. a） 会计主体假设； b） 持续经营假设； c） 会计分期假设； d） 货币计量假设； e） 历史成本原则； f） 实现原则； g） 配比原则； h） 全面披露原则
3. 1） A； 2） B； 3） D
4. 1） The function and primary focus of financial accounting is to provide useful financial in-

formation of an entity that may be helpful for information users.

2) The internal users of accounting information are managements, employees, labor unions, et al.

3) The external users of accounting information are investors, creditors, government agencies, public general, customers, suppliers.

4) The key accounting assumptions are economic entity, going concern, periodicity, and monetary unit assumption.

5) "Relevance" means that the information may be relevant to the prediction of future events, which may have impact on the decision-making process; it also means that the information is relevant in helping to confirm past events. "Reliability" is the extent to which information is verifiable, faithful and neutral. For example, the historical cost of a set of equipment to be reported in the balance sheet of a company is usually highly verifiable. The cost can be traced to an exchange transaction, the purchase of the equipment.

6) The going concern assumption assumes that the enterprise has neither the intention nor the necessity of liquidation or of curtailing materially the scale of its operations.

7) The major accounting principles include Historical Cost Principle, Realization Principle, Matching Principle and Full Disclosure Principle.

8) The main difference between cash basis model and accrual basis model is the basis of when revenue and expense are recognized. The cash basis of accounting recognizes revenues when cash is received, and expenses when they are paid. Under the accrual basis, revenues and expenses are recorded when they are earned, regardless of when the money is actually received or paid.

Exercises 3

1. Entries making

(1)

Dr. Cash	50, 000	
Cr. Capital		50, 000

(2)

Dr. Machinery	20, 000	
Cr. Cash		20, 000

(3)

Dr. Purchases 3,500

Cr. Account Payable (Kevin) 3,500

(4)

Dr. Purchases 4,000

Cr. Cash 4,000

(5)

Dr. Account Payable (Kevin) 3,500

Cr. Cash 3,500

(6)

Dr. Cash 3,600

Cr. Sales 3,600

Dr. COGS 3,000

Cr. Inventory 3,000

(7)

Dr. Wages 1,000

Cr. Cash 1,000

2. Case

1) Journalization of the preceding transactions

Accounts and Explanations		Dr.	Cr.
(1)	Cash	45,000	
	Notes payable		45,000
(2)	Land	40,000	
	Cash		40,000
(3)	Cash	5,000	
	Service revenue		5,000
(4)	Supplies	300	
	Accounts payable		300
(5)	Accounts receivable	2,600	
	Revenue		2,600
(6)	Accounts payable	1,200	
	Cash		1,200

(Continued)

Accounts and Explanations		Dr.	Cr.
(7)	Salary expense	3, 000	
	Rent expene	1, 500	
	Interest expense	400	
	Cash		4, 900
(8)	Cash	3, 100	
	Accounts receivable		3, 100
(9)	Utilities expense	200	
	Accounts payable		200
(10)	Dividends	1, 800	
	Cash		1, 800

2) Cooper Company trial balance (March 31st 2019)

Accounts Title	Dr.	Cr.
Cash	32, 200	
Accounts receivable	4, 000	
Supplies	2, 000	
Land	40, 000	
Accounts payable		3, 000
Notes payable		45, 000
Common Stock		10, 000
Dividends	1, 800	
Service revenue		7, 600
Salary expense	3, 000	
Rent expense	1, 500	
Retained earnings		19, 500
Interest expense	400	
Utilities expense	200	
Total	85, 100	85, 100

Exercises 4

1. （1）A；（2）D；（3）D；（4）D

2. （1）现金及现金等价物；（2）存货；（3）非流动资产；（4）房屋、厂房和设备；（5）无形资产；（6）商誉；（7）折旧；（8）摊销；（9）余额；（10）有价证券；（11）备用金；（12）市场（公允）价值；（13）工作量（折旧）法；（14）磨损；（15）未来经济利益

3. 1）Calculation.

（1）The cost of the machine = $36,000+ $2,000+ $1,200 = $39,200

（2）按 a）Straight-line-depreciation method（直线折旧法计算）的 2019 年折旧为：

（$39,200－$500）/ 6 = $6,450

按 b）Units-of-production-depreciation method（工作量法计算）的 2019 年折旧为：

（$39,200－$500）/ 40,000 * 6,000 = $5,805

2）Accounting entries.

（1）On Sep. 1 2019

Dr. Raw Material	5,000	
Cr. Cash		5,000

（2）On Sep. 5 2019：

Dr. Work in Process	2,000	
Cr. Raw Material		2,000

（3）On Sep. 10 2019：

Dr. Cost of Goods Sold	3,000	
Cr. Finished Goods		3,000
Dr. Cash	7,000	
Cr. Revenue		7,000

（4）At the end of Sep. 2019：

Dr. Manufacturing Overhead	4,000	
Cr. Accumulated Depreciation		4,000

（5）On Sep. 20 2019：

Dr. Intangible Asset	9,000	
Cr. Cash		9,000

（6）Amortization：

Dr. Other Expense	3,000	
Cr. Accumulated Amortization		3,000

4. (1) Assets refer to resources owned and controlled by the entity as a result of past transactions and events, from which future economic benefits are expected to flow to the entity. A key characteristic of an asset represents probable future economic benefits.

   (2) Current assets represent all the assets of a company that are expected to be sold, consumed, utilized or exhausted through the standard business operations. For example, cash, receivables, inventory.

   (3) Liquidity refers to the ease with which an asset, or security, can be converted into ready cash without affecting its market price.

   (4) The accounting process of production from raw materials to inventory includes the work in process made from raw materials, direct labor, manufacturing overhead. The work in process would be credited when it is finished.

   (5) Cash and cash equivalent are the very liquid asset, which is needed to run business for all companies.

   (6) The company which has plenty funds would have transactions of long-term investment to make the best use of its current asset.

   (7) Depreciation is the expensing of a fixed asset over its useful life. The four regular depreciation methods are straight-line depreciation (直线法折旧法), sum of years digits (年限总和法), units of production (工作量法), double declining balance (双倍余额递减法).

Exercise 5

1. (1) 流动负债

   (2) 透支

   (3) 应付票据

   (4) 应付账款

   (5) 其他应付款

   (6) 预收收入

   (7) 应付职工薪酬

   (8) 应付股利

   (9) 应付企业所得税

   (10) 销售税

   (11) 应付所得税

   (12) 长期负债

（13）长期借款
（14）债券
（15）应付债券
（16）本金
（17）利息
（18）到期日
（19）应计利息
（20）或有负债

2.（1）（d）
（2）（a）
（3）（b）
（4）（f）
（5）（c）
（6）（i）

3. C

4.（1）ABD；（2）AB

Exercise 6

1.（1）分配
（2）分割
（3）股票
（4）发行
（5）普通股
（6）优先股
（7）股东
（8）红利
（9）优先购买权
（10）票面价值股票
（11）非票面价值股票
（12）实收资本
（13）附加实收资本
（14）资本公积
（15）留存收益

(16) 现金股利
(17) 股票股利
(18) 宣布分配股利
(19) 分配股利
(20) 股票分割

2. (1) (d)
(2) (b) (i)
(3) (a) (e)
(4) (g)
(5) (f)
(6) (h)

3. (1) C; (2) C

4. (1) BC
(2) ABC
(3) ABC

5. (1) T
(2) F
(3) F
(4) F
(5) T

Exercise 7

1. (1) 销售收入
(2) 服务收入
(3) 主营业务收入
(4) 提供服务
(5) 生产成本
(6) 直接材料成本
(7) 直接人工成本
(8) 制造费用
(9) 租赁费用
(10) 维护费用
(11) 期间费用

（12）管理费用
（13）财务费用
（14）运输费用
（15）广告费用

2. （1）（a）
（2）（d）
（3）（c）（e）（g）
（4）（f）
（5）（h）
（6）（i）

3. （1）D
（2）C

4. （1）ABC
（2）AD

5. （1）T
（2）F
（3）T
（4）T
（5）F

Exercise 8

1. （1）D；（2）D；（3）B

2. （1）创办企业
（2）从银行取得贷款
（3）购买无形资产
（4）销售成本
（5）赊销
（6）产生未来现金流
（7）账面价值
（8）公允价值
（9）利润表（损益表）
（10）销售活动

Exercise 9

1.

Workings		
Gross profit margin	31, 800/52, 100 * 100%	61%
Operating profit margin	19, 588/52, 100 * 100%	38%
Receivable collection period (days)	(5, 700/52, 100) * 365	40
Current ratio	(12, 900−1, 412) /11, 600	1 : 1
Acid test (quick) ratio	(12, 900−4, 900−1, 412) /11, 600	0. 57 : 1
Gearing (debt/equity)	16, 700/ (9, 000−1, 412)	220%

2.

	20×6	20×5
ROCE	7, 500/74, 300 * 100% = 10. 1%	6, 000/53, 000 * 100% = 11. 3%
Net asset turnover	46, 500/74, 300 = 0. 63 times	28, 000/53, 000 * 100% = 0. 53 times
Gross profit margin	9, 300/46, 500 * 100% = 20. 0%	7, 200/28, 000 * 100% = 25. 7%
Operating profit margin	7, 500/46, 500 * 100% = 16. 1%	6, 000/28, 000 * 100% = 21. 4%